Microsoft® Project
2016: Part 1

Microsoft® Project 2016: Part 1

Part Number: 091062
Course Edition: 1.2

Acknowledgements

PROJECT TEAM

Author	Media Designer	Content Editor
Sunni K. Brock	Brian Sullivan	Angie French

Logical Operations wishes to thank the Logical Operations Instructor Community, and in particular Tom Allen, Elizabeth Robinson, and John Wilson for contributing their technical and instructional expertise during the creation of this course.

Notices

DISCLAIMER

While Logical Operations, Inc. takes care to ensure the accuracy and quality of these materials, we cannot guarantee their accuracy, and all materials are provided without any warranty whatsoever, including, but not limited to, the implied warranties of merchantability or fitness for a particular purpose. The name used in the data files for this course is that of a fictitious company. Any resemblance to current or future companies is purely coincidental. We do not believe we have used anyone's name in creating this course, but if we have, please notify us and we will change the name in the next revision of the course. Logical Operations is an independent provider of integrated training solutions for individuals, businesses, educational institutions, and government agencies. The use of screenshots, photographs of another entity's products, or another entity's product name or service in this book is for editorial purposes only. No such use should be construed to imply sponsorship or endorsement of the book by nor any affiliation of such entity with Logical Operations. This courseware may contain links to sites on the Internet that are owned and operated by third parties (the "External Sites"). Logical Operations is not responsible for the availability of, or the content located on or through, any External Site. Please contact Logical Operations if you have any concerns regarding such links or External Sites.

TRADEMARK NOTICES

Microsoft® Project 2016: Part 1

About This Course

Welcome to *Microsoft® Project 2016: Part 1*. This course is designed to familiarize you with the basic features and functions of Microsoft Project Professional 2016 so you can use it effectively and efficiently in a real-world environment.

This course covers the critical knowledge and skills a project manager needs to create a project plan with Project 2016 during the planning phase of a project. In other words, if your supervisor assigns you to lead a project, this course will enable you to draft a project plan with Project 2016 and share it with your supervisor (and others) for review and approval.

Course Description

Target Student

This course is designed for a person with an understanding of project management concepts and who is responsible for creating and maintaining project plans. The course will give the student a fundamental understanding of Microsoft Project 2016 necessary to create and save project plans.

Course Prerequisites

To ensure your success in this course, you should have basic project management knowledge and skills. The following Logical Operations course can help you in meeting this requirement: *Project Management Fundamentals (Second Edition)*.

You should also have basic knowledge and skills for using any current Windows® operating system—preferably Windows 10. The following Logical Operations courses can help you meet this requirement:

- *Using Microsoft® Windows® 10*
- *Microsoft® Windows® 10: Transition from Windows® 7*

Finally, you should have competency in using other Microsoft Office applications—preferably Office 2016. You can take any of the Office 2016 course offerings from Logical Operations to attain the requisite knowledge and skills.

Course Objectives

In this course, you will learn to create and engage in basic management of a project using Microsoft Project Professional 2016.

You will:

- Identify project management concepts and navigate the Project 2016 environment.
- Create and define a new project plan.
- Create and organize tasks.

- Manage resources in a project plan.
- Finalize a project plan.

The CHOICE Home Screen

Logon and access information for your CHOICE environment will be provided with your class experience. The CHOICE platform is your entry point to the CHOICE learning experience, of which this course manual is only one part.

On the CHOICE Home screen, you can access the CHOICE Course screens for your specific courses. Visit the CHOICE Course screen both during and after class to make use of the world of support and instructional resources that make up the CHOICE experience.

Each CHOICE Course screen will give you access to the following resources:

- **Classroom**: A link to your training provider's classroom environment.
- **eBook**: An interactive electronic version of the printed book for your course.
- **Files**: Any course files available to download.
- **Checklists**: Step-by-step procedures and general guidelines you can use as a reference during and after class.
- **LearnTOs**: Brief animated videos that enhance and extend the classroom learning experience.
- **Assessment**: A course assessment for your self-assessment of the course content.
- Social media resources that enable you to collaborate with others in the learning community using professional communications sites such as LinkedIn or microblogging tools such as Twitter.

Depending on the nature of your course and the components chosen by your learning provider, the CHOICE Course screen may also include access to elements such as:

- LogicalLABS, a virtual technical environment for your course.
- Various partner resources related to the courseware.
- Related certifications or credentials.
- A link to your training provider's website.
- Notices from the CHOICE administrator.
- Newsletters and other communications from your learning provider.
- Mentoring services.

Visit your CHOICE Home screen often to connect, communicate, and extend your learning experience!

How to Use This Book

As You Learn

This book is divided into lessons and topics, covering a subject or a set of related subjects. In most cases, lessons are arranged in order of increasing proficiency.

The results-oriented topics include relevant and supporting information you need to master the content. Each topic has various types of activities designed to enable you to solidify your understanding of the informational material presented in the course. Information is provided for reference and reflection to facilitate understanding and practice.

Data files for various activities as well as other supporting files for the course are available by download from the CHOICE Course screen. In addition to sample data for the course exercises, the course files may contain media components to enhance your learning and additional reference materials for use both during and after the course.

Checklists of procedures and guidelines can be used during class and as after-class references when you're back on the job and need to refresh your understanding.

t the back of the book, you will find a glossary of the definitions of the terms and concepts used throughout the course. You will also find an index to assist in locating information within the instructional components of the book. In many electronic versions of the book, you can click links on key words in the content to move to the associated glossary definition, and on page references in the index to move to that term in the content. To return to the previous location in the document after clicking a link, use the appropriate functionality in your PDF viewing software.

As You Review

Any method of instruction is only as effective as the time and effort you, the student, are willing to invest in it. In addition, some of the information that you learn in class may not be important to you immediately, but it may become important later. For this reason, we encourage you to spend some time reviewing the content of the course after your time in the classroom.

As a Reference

The organization and layout of this book make it an easy-to-use resource for future reference. Taking advantage of the glossary, index, and table of contents, you can use this book as a first source of definitions, background information, and summaries.

Course Icons

Watch throughout the material for the following visual cues.

Icon	Description
	A **Note** provides additional information, guidance, or hints about a topic or task.
	A **Caution** note makes you aware of places where you need to be particularly careful with your actions, settings, or decisions so that you can be sure to get the desired results of an activity or task.
	LearnTO notes show you where an associated LearnTO is particularly relevant to the content. Access LearnTOs from your CHOICE Course screen.
	Checklists provide job aids you can use after class as a reference to perform skills back on the job. Access checklists from your CHOICE Course screen.
	Social notes remind you to check your CHOICE Course screen for opportunities to interact with the CHOICE community using social media.

1 Getting Started with Microsoft Project

Lesson Time: 45 minutes

Lesson Introduction

As a project manager, you need to create and manage many documents (artifacts) to communicate the project's purpose and status. A key component of this responsibility is the project plan, which incorporates the tasks, resources, and scheduling of a project. Not only should the project plan be used in the initial phases of a project, but also keeping a plan up-to-date as the project progresses enables you to effectively manage the project and communicate status to all involved parties.

Microsoft® Project Professional 2016 is a powerful tool for planning and managing projects. This lesson will provide you with the big picture—some basic knowledge and skills you need to start using Project 2016.

The lesson starts with a brief review of basic project management concepts. The remainder of the lesson is presented as if Microsoft Project Professional 2016 had just been installed on your computer and you are running it for the first time. It will cover the essentials you need to navigate the program. In later lessons, you will add to this framework.

Lesson Objectives

In this lesson, you will navigate the Project environment. You will:

- Identify project management concepts and project phases.
- Navigate the Microsoft Project Professional 2016 interface.

TOPIC A

Identify Project Management Concepts

As a project manager, you have to manage and control your project to make it a success. Whether you are a beginning project manager, or a seasoned professional, you need to understand project management concepts and apply them as they relate to the application. Regardless of your project management experience and training, this topic reviews some basic project management concepts in the common terminology so that you can better understand Microsoft Project Professional 2016.

Projects

A *project* is a temporary initiative to create a unique result. Every project has a definite starting point and ending point in time. When the desired result has been achieved, the project is over. Here are some project examples:

- A company engages in a 10-month project to develop a new tablet computer.
- A county government implements a three-year project to construct four dog parks.
- A nonprofit organization engages in a six-week project to increase membership by 10 percent.

Project Process Groups

There are five project management process groups during which specific project management activities occur.

Process Group	Activities
Initiating	The project's goal is defined and the project is authorized. The output of this process is often a project charter.
Planning	The project's scope, time, cost, and other details are determined. The output of this process is a project plan.
Executing	Tasks are performed and resources are utilized to accomplish the project plan.
Monitoring and Controlling	The project's progress is tracked and corrective action is taken when necessary to keep the project on track.
Closing	The project's products, services, or end results are accepted by those who authorized the project, and the project is brought to an orderly conclusion.

The project management process groups relate to one another as shown in the following figure.

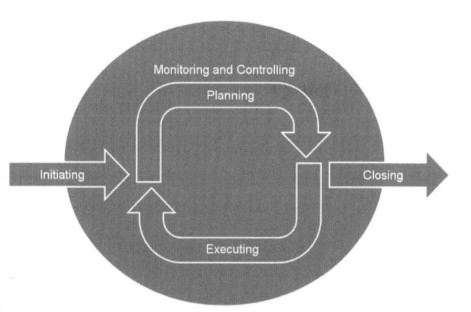

Figure 1-1: The five project management process groups.

As you may have noticed, the Planning and Executing process groups are a continuous cycle. As the project plan is executed, more planning is often required. Also, you may have noticed that the Monitoring and Controlling process group interfaces with and affects the other four groups.

 Note: Microsoft Project Professional 2016 is designed to help you with the Planning, Executing, and Monitoring and Controlling process groups of project management.

Project Constraints

Project constraints are anything that constrains or dictates the actions of the project team. Scope, Time, and Cost are the most important constraints. In fact, they are referred to as the *triple constraints*. These knowledge areas are dynamically linked; any change in one will impact the others. Project 2016 is intended to help project managers deal with various project constraints.

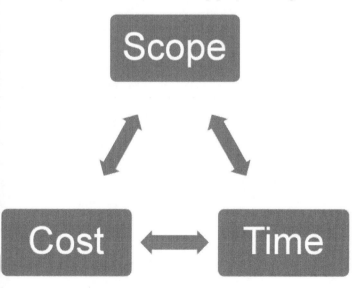

Figure 1-2: The triple constraints of a project are dynamically linked; you cannot change one without changing another.

Scope Creep

Project managers must be constantly on guard against *scope creep*, which is the uncontrolled expansion of a project's scope. A multitude of seemingly minor scope changes can add up to major time delays and cost overruns.

Project Management

Project management is the administration and supervision of projects using a well-defined set of knowledge, skills, tools, and techniques. Project management is both a science and an art that—when done properly—ensures projects are completed on time, within budget, and according to specifications.

Some project managers undergo a rigorous process to become certified by the Project Management Institute (PMI®) as a Project Management Professional (PMP®). Other project managers find themselves performing this job function with little or no formal training. Whether you are a project management novice or master, Microsoft Project Professional 2016 is a powerful tool that will help you plan and complete your projects successfully.

 Note: The authoritative source for project management information and best practices is *A Guide to the Project Management Body of Knowledge (PMBOK® Guide)*, which is maintained by PMI. It is an invaluable reference for anyone who manages projects. Visit **www.pmi.org** for more information.

Project Roles

Projects often require a group of people with different roles and responsibilities to communicate with each other and work together. The cohesiveness of this group can affect the project's successful completion.

Role	Description
project manager	The primary person directing the project's flow and the communication between project participants. The project manager leads the planning of the project, watches for cost overruns, and manages disputes.
project sponsor	The person in your organization who authorizes, supports, and approves the project. Usually, the project sponsor is a member of senior management.
project stakeholder	Anyone who is actively involved in the project or has an interest in its outcome. Stakeholders can be inside your organization or outside of it. For example, if the project is to drill a hydraulic fracturing well, internal stakeholders might include geologists, construction workers, and drill operators. External stakeholders might include landowners, environmental groups, and government regulators.
team member	A person who is responsible for performing or approving the work to complete the project. This includes the people who work on the tasks, referred to as human resources, such as engineers or operators, and may also include resource managers, such as a foreman or director.

ACTIVITY 1–1
Identifying Project Management Concepts

Scenario

Use these questions to check your knowledge of project management concepts.

---

1. True or False? A project is a series of steps performed to reach a specific goal.

   ☐ True

   ☐ False

2. The scope, the tasks involved, and the resources required for a project are all defined during which process group?

   ○ Executing

   ○ Monitoring and Controlling

   ○ Closing

   ○ Planning

3. What is the importance of monitoring a project?

4. True or False? Project management is the application of knowledge, skills, tools, and techniques to accomplish activities or tasks to meet the objectives set for a project.

   ☐ True

   ☐ False

5. Which project management process group involves the completion of tasks and the coordination of people and other resources to carry out the plan?

   ○ Initiating

   ○ Executing

   ○ Planning

   ○ Closing

6. Who is the project sponsor?

7. **Which of the following are considered the classic triple constraints?**

☐ Scope

☐ Cost

☐ Earned Value

☐ Time

☐ Space

8. **What is scope creep?**

_____

TOPIC B

Navigate the Microsoft Project 2016 Environment

Now that you have reviewed some basic information about project management, you can start to work with Microsoft Project Professional 2016. If you are new to Microsoft Project, a good first step is to launch the application and explore the interface and its functions before you begin using it to develop live project plans. In this topic, you will navigate the Microsoft Project Professional 2016 interface to become familiar with the program's basic features.

It is essential to identify the various elements of any new application you are using for the first time. By identifying the different components in the Microsoft Project 2016 interface, you can be at ease with its features and functions and then work more efficiently on your project plan files.

Microsoft Project 2016

Microsoft Project 2016 is an application that is part of the Microsoft Office 2016 suite of user-productivity software. Project is a powerful project management program that enables you to create, present, manipulate, manage, and analyze project plans. Project's extensive features give you control over a project's schedule, tasks, and resources. This detailed management of a project will help you ensure that your projects are successful and make the best uses of time and resources.

The Start Screen

The **Start** screen is the first screen you see when you open Microsoft Project Professional 2016. The **Start** screen contains multiple options to help you get started with using Project.

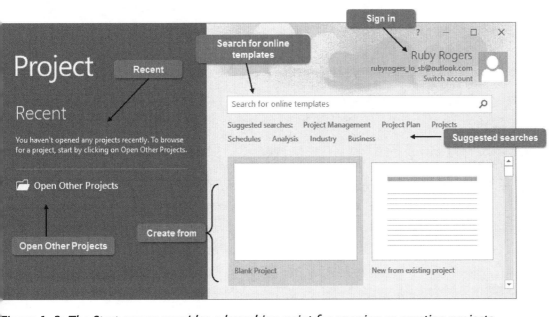

Figure 1-3: The Start screen provides a launching point for opening or creating projects.

From this screen you can use the following commands.

Command	Description
Recent	Click on the name of a recent project file to open it.

Command	Description
Open Other Projects	Open other Project files that are not on the **Recent** list.
Search for online templates	Search online for Project templates that you can use to start a new Projec file.
Suggested searches	Use suggested keywords to browse Project templates.
Create from	Choose to create a new blank project file, a new project from an existing file, or a new project from a template.
Sign in	Log in to your Microsoft account.

 Note: You may already have a personal or organizational Microsoft account. Examples of personal Microsoft accounts include Office 365, Skype®, OneDrive®, Xbox LIVE®, and Outlook.com. If you don't have a Microsoft account, you can create one for free at **http:// signup.live.com.**

Views

Microsoft Project 2016 uses *views* to display information on the screen from the currently open project plan file. You can use a variety of views to focus on specific aspects of your project. These might include **Gantt Chart** view, **Network Diagram** view, **Calendar** view, **Resource Sheet** view, and **Resource Usage** view. Most views are separated into two panes—with the **Sheet** pane on the left and the **Chart** pane on the right.

The Gantt Chart View

The *Gantt Chart* is the default view in Microsoft Project 2016. When you first open a blank projec Project displays this view. Gantt charts are the most common method for displaying project information.

In the right pane of the **Gantt Chart** view, you will see the duration of each task plotted as a bar against the dates along the top of the pane.

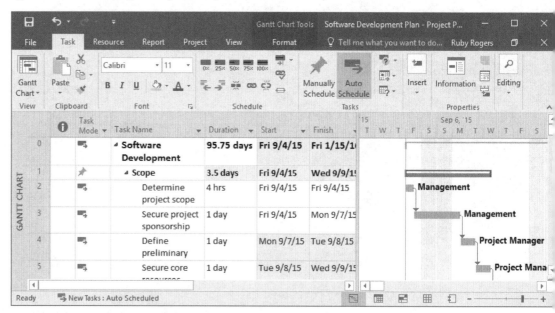

Figure 1-4: The Gantt Chart view is where you will spend most of your time working with a project plan.

Note: The Gantt chart is named after Henry Gantt, who designed this tool between 1910 and 1915. Although now regarded as a common charting technique, Gantt charts were considered revolutionary when first introduced.

The View Bar

Selecting a button on the **View Bar** changes what is displayed in the view. The most commonly used **View** buttons are shown at the top of the **View Bar.** You can see additional **View** buttons by selecting the down arrow at the bottom of the **View Bar.**

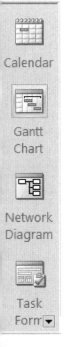

Figure 1-5: The View Bar enables you to quickly change between the most used views.

The Quick Access Toolbar

In the top-left corner of the window you will see the *Quick Access Toolbar.* As its name implies, the toolbar enables you to rapidly perform those Microsoft Project Professional 2016 commands that you use most often—such as **Save, Undo,** and **Redo.**

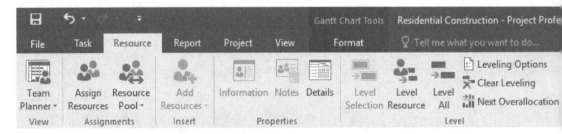

Figure 1-6: The Quick Access Toolbar is highly customizable and always available on the screen.

The Ribbon

The *ribbon* at the top of the window is where you will find most of the controls used in Microsoft Project Professional 2016. The controls are grouped into six basic tabs:

- **File**
- **Task**
- **Resource**
- **Report**
- **Project**
- **View**

When you select a tab, the controls related to that tab are displayed on the ribbon. A different default view button will be shown on the far left of the ribbon for each tab. For example, the **Gantt Chart** view button is the default for the **Task** tab, and the **Team Planner** view button is the default for the **Resource** tab.

Figure 1-7: The ribbon groups the most common commands into tabs by type.

Note: This course uses a streamlined notation for ribbon commands. They'll appear as "[Ribbon Tab]→[Group]→[Button or Control]" as in "Select **Task**→**Clipboard**→**Paste**." If the group name isn't needed for navigation or there isn't a group, it's omitted, as in "Select **File**→**Open**." For selections that open menus and submenus, this notation convention will continue until you are directed to select the final command or option, as in "Select **Task**→**Editing**→**Clear**→**Clear All**."

Note: Some Project 2016 command buttons are split, meaning there are actually two separate buttons you can select independently. This is often the case with commands that have multiple options/variations accessible by selecting a drop-down arrow. The **Paste** command button in the **Clipboard** group on the **Task** tab is an example of this. For these commands, you will be directed to either select just the button, as in "Select **Task→Clipboard→Paste**," or you will be directed to select the drop-down arrow if necessary, as in "Select **Task→Clipboard→Paste drop-down arrow→Paste Special**."

The Backstage

The **File** tab displays differently than the other tabs. When you select it, you will see the *Backstage*—where you can access a number of file and program controls. The **Backstage** provides a central location for commands used to take action on a project as a whole, such as creating a file, saving a file, and preparing to print.

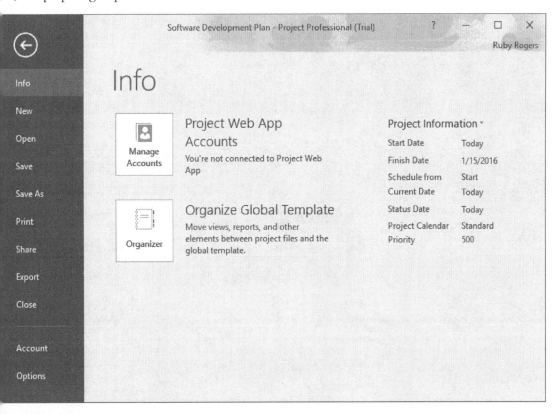

Figure 1-8: The Backstage enables you to work with project files and program settings.

The Contextual Tab

In addition to the six basic tabs, the ribbon also contains a *contextual tab*. This tab changes names and colors depending on what is selected in the view. When you select this tab, you will see all of the tools related to the currently selected pane or object in one place on the ribbon. For example, when you work in **Gantt Chart** view, the ribbon displays the **Gantt Chart Tools | Format** tab. If you switch to **Resource Sheet** view, the ribbon will display the **Resource Sheet Tools | Format** tab. The commands and options on the **Format** tab change the most from view to view, while the other tabs show dimmed (unavailable) commands if they cannot be used in the current view.

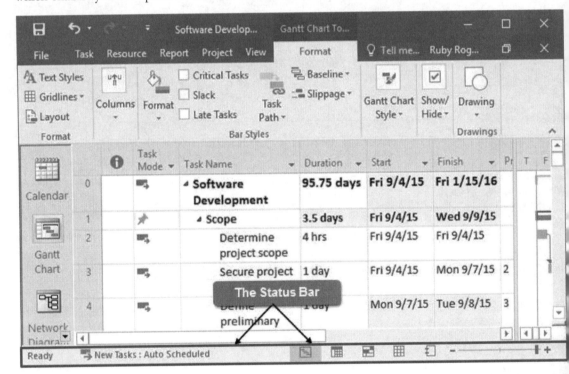

Figure 1-9: The Contextual tab adapts to what you are doing in the view area.

The Status Bar

The *status bar* at the bottom of the window shows you some of the current program settings. It also displays shortcuts to the most commonly used views. Finally, it contains the **Zoom** control, which enables you to expand or contract the time scale shown in the view.

Figure 1-10: The Status bar shows you current program status and enables you to quickly change views and zoom levels.

 Note: If you use Project with Microsoft Project Server or SharePoint, the status bar will also show you status notifications from the server.

The Tell Me Bar

Type into the *Tell Me bar* to quickly access commands just like a search command. The most commonly used commands and tasks are shown at the top of the results list. You can see additional help by selecting **Get Help on** at the bottom of the list.

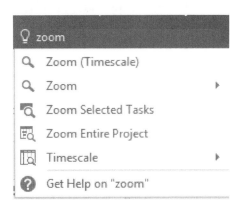

Figure 1-11: *The Tell Me bar, new to Project 2016, is designed to help you find commands quickly.*

Access the Checklist tile on your CHOICE Course screen for reference information and job aids on How to Navigate the Project 2016 Interface.

ACTIVITY 1-2
Navigating the Project 2016 Interface

Before You Begin

Microsoft Project Professional 2016 is installed on your computer and activated.

Scenario

Building with Heart is a non-profit home construction organization whose purpose is to build famil homes for qualifying applicants using recycled materials and volunteer labor when possible.

You joined Building with Heart as a volunteer project manager. The organization received a donation of new Microsoft software and you have just installed Microsoft Project Professional 201(on your laptop. You begin to familiarize yourself with the program and identify the features you wi use most often.

> **Note:** Activities may vary slightly if the software vendor has issued digital updates. Your instructor will notify you of any changes.

1. **Open Microsoft Project Professional 2016.**
   a) On the Windows 10 **Start** menu, select **All apps**, and find the **Project 2016** tile.

   b) Right-click the **Project 2016** tile and select **More→Pin to taskbar**.
   c) On the taskbar, select **Project 2016**.
      Verify that Project 2016 opens to the **Start** screen.

2. **Start a new project.**
   a) On the Project 2016 **Start** screen, in the **Search for online templates** field, type the search term
      simple, and select the **Start Searching** button.
   b) From the search results, select **Simple project plan**.
   c) Select **Create**.
      Verify that a new **Simple project plan** opens.

3. **Explore the ribbon.**
   a) On the ribbon, select the **Task** tab (if it isn't already selected). Move the mouse pointer over each button on the **Task** tab to reveal and read a **ScreenTip** that explains the button's function.
   b) Explore the other tabs and their buttons in the same manner.

4. **Zoom the time scale to the entire project using the Tell Me bar.**
   a) In the **Tell Me** bar, type *zoom*
   b) In the results list, select **Zoom Entire Project**.
      Verify that the time scale for the entire project fits the width of the Gantt chart's right pane.

5. **Make the View Bar visible.**
   a) On the left side of the screen, right-click the view name (such as **GANTT CHART**).
   b) From the menu, select **View Bar**.

Confirm that the **View Bar** is now visible.

Locate the commands on the **View Bar** that you will use the most.

a) On the **View Bar,** select **Calendar.**
b) Verify that the **Calendar** view displays.
c) Locate the remaining buttons on the **View Bar** and verify the views displayed. Scroll down if necessary to see more commands.

Add a print command to the **Quick Access Toolbar.**

a) On the right side of the **Quick Access Toolbar,** select **Customize Quick Access Toolbar.**
b) Select **Print Preview**.

Verify that **Print Preview** appears on the **Quick Access Toolbar.**

Close Microsoft Project Professional 2016 without saving the file.

a) On the top-right corner of the **Project Professional** window, select the **Close** button.
b) In the **Microsoft Project** dialog box, select **No** to discard the changes.
Verify that Project 2016 is closed.

Summary

In this lesson, you started using Microsoft Project Professional 2016. By reviewing the basics of project management and navigating the Project interface, you laid the foundation for the knowledg and skills that will enable you to use Project effectively.

What is your next big project—either at work or at home?

How do you think Microsoft Project 2016 could help you with planning your project?

 Note: Check your CHOICE Course screen for opportunities to interact with your classmates, peers, and the larger CHOICE online community about the topics covered in this course or other topics you are interested in. From the Course screen you can also access available resources for a more continuous learning experience.

2 | Defining a Project

Lesson Time: 1 hour

Lesson Introduction

Defining a new project encompasses all the steps that a project manager needs to take in Microsoft® Project Professional 2016 to ensure that the new project plan has the necessary information before the task planning process begins. Capturing the information about the project that you discovered in the Initiating process is important so that anyone looking at your plan understands what the project is about. This is helpful to even you, if you must put it aside and come back later. Any project manager, whether new or very experienced, can save time and effort down the road by taking advantage of pre-defined project plan structures for common project types so that they don't have to start from scratch. Building a well-defined project plan library over time is key to increasing your skills and efficiency on future projects.

By creating a new project plan, and taking the time to enter the appropriate information correctly and set up your calendars, you will lay the foundation for a sustainable project plan that is easier to build, maintain, and share over the course of your project.

Lesson Objectives

In this lesson, you will define a project. You will:

- Create a new project plan and identify options for creating a new plan.

- Define the project level options and project description.

- Modify and assign project calendars.

TOPIC A

Create a New Project Plan

Now that you're familiar with common project management concepts, and know your way around the Microsoft Project 2016 interface, you're ready to start managing a project. In order to take full advantage of the robust capabilities of Project, it stands to reason that you must first create a project plan in the application. In this topic, you'll do just that.

Methods for Creating New Projects

Defining a new project begins with creating a new project plan file. You can begin with a blank file or start with a template that is already populated with project phases and tasks for common project types. When you first open the application, Project displays the **Start** screen, which gives you several methods for creating new files.

Figure 2-1: You can choose from five methods for creating new projects.

The following table describes the different methods for creating new project plan files.

Method	Description
Blank Project	This method gives you a completely empty file into which you can add all of your project information.
New from an existing project	This method enables you to reuse a Project file from a previous project.
New from Excel® workbook	This method imports project information created in Excel. When you choose this option, a wizard will open and guide you though the steps of importing the project information from Excel to Project.
New from SharePoint® Tasks	This method enables you to import project information from a SharePoint task list. When you choose this option, you will be prompted to enter a SharePoint URL and select a task list on the SharePoint site.

Method	Description
From a Project template	This method enables you to create a Project file that is customized for a variety of different project types. When you choose this option, a Project file containing sample information will be created. You can then modify the information for your particular project.

Note: Microsoft SharePoint is a web-based application that enables geographically distributed teams to store, sync, and share their important content. Visit **http://sharepoint.microsoft.com/** to learn more about SharePoint.

Project Templates

A *project template* contains details for a sample project that you can edit to make your own or simply use to help frame your own project phases.

Microsoft Project Professional 2016 comes preloaded with twelve templates that are geared toward a variety of different project types. Using a template can save you time because you do not have to create the project structure from scratch. However, you will still need to modify the template with the details of your particular project. If you do not see a template on the **Start** screen that is similar to your project, you can search online for one that is.

Residential Construction Market Research Schedule New Business Plan SOX Compliance and Tec...

Six Sigma DMAIC Cycle Customer Service Annual Report Preparati... Merger or Acquisition E...

Figure 2-2: Project templates help you create new project plans with much of the information and formatting in place.

Access the Checklist tile on your CHOICE Course screen for reference information and job aids on How to Create a New Project Plan.

ACTIVITY 2–1
Creating a New Project Plan

Before You Begin
Microsoft Project Professional 2016 is installed on your machine.

Scenario
Building with Heart, located in Greene City, is a non-profit home construction organization similar to Habitat for Humanity. The Building with Heart program's purpose is to build a two- or three-bedroom home for each qualifying family. These homes have a mortgage with a very reasonable interest rate, and because many materials and labor are donated, the mortgage is much less than if everything had to be purchased outright.

As a volunteer project manager at Building with Heart, you have just started a new construction project to build a new three-bedroom home for a qualifying family whose previous residence was destroyed by a storm. You need to create a new project plan for the project. Instead of starting from a blank project plan, you want to find a template that will help you create your construction project plan more quickly.

1. Open Microsoft Project Professional 2016.

   a) On the taskbar, select the **Project 2016** shortcut.
      Verify that Project 2016 opens to the **Start** screen.

2. Create a new construction project.

   a) On the Project 2016 **Start** screen, in the **Search for online templates** field, type the search term *construction* and select the **Start Searching** button.
   b) From the search results, select **Residential Construction**.
   c) In the **Residential Construction** dialog box, in the **Start Date** field, enter or select the date that corresponds to next Monday.
   d) Select **Create**.
      Verify that Project opens a new **Residential Construction** project plan, and leave the file open.

TOPIC B

Define a Project

After creating a new project plan, it is important to capture the information about your project and save it so that you and others can easily understand what the project is about. In this topic, you will define your project plan by entering the information and setting options specific to your project, and then you will save your new file.

The Project Information Dialog Box

When you create a project file, you are not prompted to supply any project information. A good place to get started is the *Project Information dialog box*. The **Project Information** dialog box captures high-level information about your project as a whole. By default, the **Project Information** dialog box uses the current date as the project start date. Project calculates the finish date after all of your task information is established and linked.

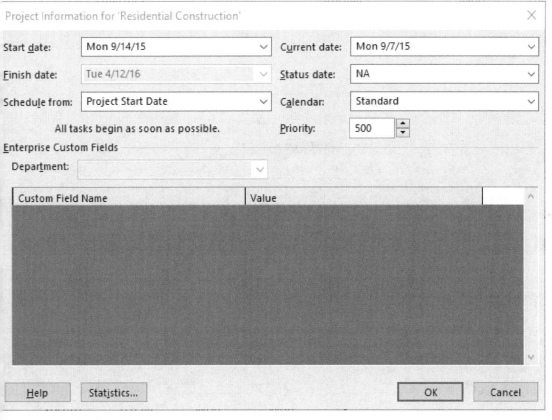

Figure 2–3: The place to view and modify high–level information about your project is the Project Information dialog box.

The Project Properties Dialog Box

In the *Project Properties dialog box*, you can enter general project information, such as the project name, the project manager's name, the name of your organization, and specific keywords related to the project. This information will help you organize and locate your project files.

Figure 2-4: The Project Properties dialog box.

 Note: Filling in the project name and keywords in the **Project Properties** dialog box will help search indexing on your local machine and in other shared file scenarios such as when using SharePoint. It will help you and others in your organization find the project plan using the **Search** command in Windows or SharePoint.

Methods for Scheduling Projects

The project's beginning date is shown in the **Start date** field of the **Project Information** dialog box. The project's ending date is shown in the **Finish date** field. You can change the **Start date** or **Finish date** by selecting the down arrow on the right side of each field.

Project Information for 'Residential Construction'   ✕

Start date:	Mon 9/14/15 ⌄	Current date:	Mon 9/7/15 ⌄
Finish date:	Tue 4/12/16 ⌄	Status date:	NA ⌄
Schedule from:	Project Start Date ⌄	Calendar:	Standard ⌄

       Project Start Date
All tas Project Finish Date   Priority: 500 ⏶⏷

Enterprise Custom Fields

Department: ⌄

Custom Field Name	Value	⌃
		⌄

Help	Statistics...		OK	Cancel

Figure 2-5: Scheduling a project from the start date or finish date.

Projects can be scheduled either from a start date or a finish date (but not both at the same time). The **Schedule from** drop-down list in the **Project Information** dialog box shows whether your project is scheduled from the start date or the finish date. If the **Schedule from** drop-down list is set to **Project Start Date,** the **Start date** drop-down list will be active and the **Finish date** drop-down list will be inactive. On the other hand, if the **Schedule from** drop-down list is set to **Project Finish Date,** the **Finish date** drop-down list will be active and the **Start date** drop-down list will be inactive.

By default, Microsoft Project 2016 schedules all new projects from a start date. In this mode, all tasks are automatically scheduled to begin as soon as possible, giving the maximum amount of schedule flexibility.

Guidelines for Scheduling a Project from the Finish Date

If you choose to schedule a project from a finish date, all new tasks will be automatically scheduled to begin as late as possible. This constraint, as well as others that may be applied in this mode, limit schedule flexibility. It is advantageous to schedule a project from a finish date when:

Your project has a firm deadline and you want to identify a date when the project must start in order to finish on time.

You are not sure when your project will begin.

Your organization requires that this mode be used.

It is better for the project to start as late as possible.

Note: If the **Schedule from** drop-down list is set to **Project Finish Date** during the planning phase of your project, consider changing **Schedule from** to **Project Start Date** during implementation. This will increase your flexibility to make schedule changes if necessary.

Current Date Changes

If necessary, you can change the project's current date in the **Current date** field of the **Project Information** dialog box. Normally, you will keep the current date the same as the actual date. However, sometimes you may want Project 2016 to act as if the current date is a different date from the actual date. For example, if you are planning for a future project, you may want to make the current date the same as the start date.

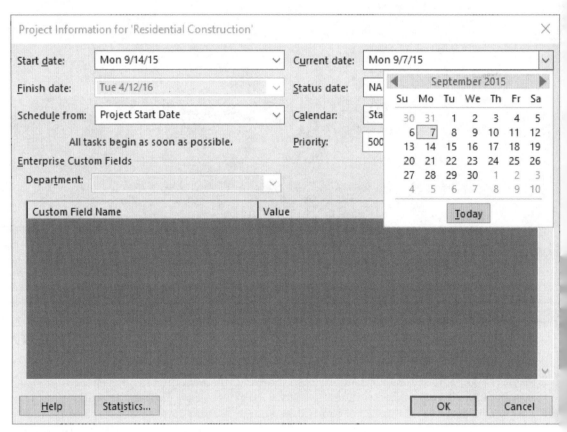

Figure 2-6: You can change the date that Project uses as the Current date.

The Save As Screen

You can save a new Microsoft Project Professional 2016 file by selecting the **File** tab on the ribbon and then selecting the **Save As** tab on the **Backstage.** You have the option of saving your Project 2016 file in three different places.

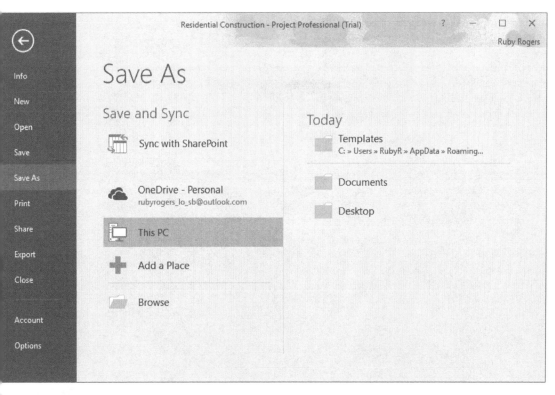

Figure 2–7: You can choose where to save a project plan on the Save As screen.

Place	Description
Sync with SharePoint	This option saves and syncs your Project file on a SharePoint site. This is a good option to use if you created the project file from a SharePoint task list and your project team is utilizing SharePoint.
OneDrive	This option saves your Project file in the cloud. This is a good option to use if you need to access your Project file from more than one computer. It also means you can retrieve your Project file if your computer is damaged, lost, or stolen.
This PC	This options saves your Project file to your computer or network.

Note: If you save your Project files to OneDrive, be aware that you must have Microsoft Project 2016 installed on any computer you plan to use to access the file. For example, if you plan to access a Project file using your work computer and your home computer, both computers must have Microsoft Project 2016.

More About OneDrive

OneDrive is Microsoft's cloud-based storage service. By default, Office 2016 will save your work to your OneDrive account. When you save your files to your OneDrive account, you'll be able to access those files on any Internet-connected device with a web browser or the OneDrive app. OneDrive provides access to any files you save to it, including any Office files, photos, and more. You can view all files, or you can narrow your view to recent files you've worked on or files you've shared with specific individuals. You can even group contacts and share files at the group level.

Depending upon the level of service you purchase, your OneDrive or Office 365 account can be associated with a SharePoint server, enabling you to host your files and apps with the full power of SharePoint. SharePoint is a Microsoft platform designed to enable collaboration, file sharing, and rapid web development and deployment of applications and data.

Note: For more information on SharePoint Server, visit **http:// sharepoint.microsoft.com/en-us/preview/sharepoint.aspx.**

 Note: To further explore saving Project 2016 files to OneDrive, you can access the LearnTO **Save Project Files to OneDrive** presentation from the **LearnTO** tile on the CHOICE Course screen.

 Access the Checklist tile on your CHOICE Course screen for reference information and job aids on How to Define and Save a Project.

ACTIVITY 2-2
Defining and Saving a Project

Before You Begin
Project Professional 2016 should be running on the desktop with the unsaved **Residential Construction** project open.

Scenario
Now that you have created a new project plan for your residential construction project, you need to make some updates to it. You have received word from the funding advisor that your project will begin in May of 2016 and that the qualifying family, the Woods, have been approved for the new home. The clearing of the debris from their lot is also included in the project. You also learn that the Woods have two daughters, 12 and 9, who are excited to each be getting their own new bedroom and a shared bathroom. Greene City Interiors has agreed to donate the time of an interior designer to help the Woods choose their finishing touches. Teresa Sanchez, a respected business leader in Greene City, has also announced that she will be joining Building with Heart as a director, and you will be reporting progress to her going forward.

You capture this information in your project plan and save it.

---

1. Change the project's **Start date** and **Current Date**.
   a) On the ribbon, select **Project→Project Information**.
      Verify that the **Project Information for 'Residential Construction'** dialog box opens.
   b) In the **Start date** box, enter or select *May 2, 2016*
   c) In the **Current date** box, enter or select *May 2, 2016*
   d) Ensure that the **Schedule from** drop-down list is set to **Project Start Date**.
   e) Select **OK**.
      Verify that the dates displayed in the **Gantt Chart** view reflect the new **Start date**.

2. Update the properties of the project with your new information.
   a) On the ribbon, select **File→Info**.
   b) Select **Project Information** and then select **Advanced Properties**.
      Verify that the **Residential Construction Properties** dialog box opens.
   c) Select the **Summary** tab if it is not already selected.

d) In the text fields, enter the appropriate information as depicted in the following image:

Residential Construction Properties	?	✕

General | **Summary** | Statistics | Contents | Custom

Title: Woods Family 3BR Home

Subject: Residential Construction

Author: My Name

Manager: Teresa Sanchez

Company: Building with Heart

Category:

Keywords: residential home Woods

Comments: Clear debris. Two girls. Greene City Interiors for finishing.

Hyperlink base:

Template: Residential Construction

☐ Save preview picture

OK | Cancel

e) Select **OK**.

3. Save the file as *C:\091062Data\Defining a Project\My_Woods_3BR_Home_Project.mpp*

a) On the ribbon, select **File→Save As**.

b) Select **Browse** and then navigate to C:\091062Data\Defining a Project\.

c) In the **File name** field, enter *My_Woods_3BR_Home_Project* and select **Save**.

TOPIC C

Assign a Project Calendar

When you create a new project plan, Microsoft Project 2016 assumes that your project tasks will be performed during a standard work week. In reality, however, your project tasks may be performed during a longer or shorter work week. You may also have to take into account holidays and vacation schedules. In this topic, you will modify the project calendars in Microsoft Project 2016 so that they reflect the realities of your particular project.

Project Calendars

Microsoft Project 2016 uses calendars to determine when to schedule tasks and when resources will be available to perform work. The *project calendar* is the calendar that determines the overall schedule of a project. For example, if you have defined your organization's holidays in the project calendar, the end date that Project calculates for your project will automatically adjust so that your project will end on a workday. Although the project calendar applies to the project as a whole, you can also assign calendars to individual resources or tasks.

Base Calendars

A *base calendar* defines the working days and working hours in a calendar that can be assigned to the project. The **Project Information** dialog box shows the base calendar assigned to your project in the **Calendar** field. Microsoft Project 2016 gives you three built-in base calendars from which to choose:

Base Calendar	Description
Standard	8:00 AM to 12:00 PM
	1:00 PM to 5:00 PM
	Monday through Friday
Night Shift	12:00 AM to 3:00 AM
	4:00 AM to 8:00 AM
	11:00 PM to 12:00 AM
	Tuesday through Friday
	12:00 AM to 3:00 AM
	4:00 AM to 8:00 AM
	Saturday
24 Hours	24 hours a day
	7 days a week

The Standard base calendar is the default for all new files in Microsoft Project 2016. You can change the base calendar to one of the other options in the **Calendar** drop-down list.

The Create New Base Calendar Dialog Box

You can use the *Create New Base Calendar dialog box* to create a new base calendar for your project by copying an existing base calendar and then changing it to fit your needs. You can access the **Create New Base Calendar** dialog box by selecting the **Change Working Time** button from the **Project** tab, and then selecting **Create New Calendar**.

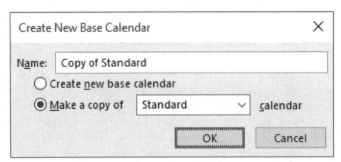

Figure 2–8: Copy a base calendar using the Create New Base Calendar dialog box.

 Note: Make sure to name your calendars descriptively so they are easy to choose later.

The Change Working Time Dialog Box

Every organization has its own working hours. If your organization's working and nonworking hours differ from the default hours of the base calendar, you can create a base calendar and apply it to the project. To plan your project accurately, you'll also need to specify any holidays that your company observes—the default base calendar does not include holidays.

Working time is whenever labor is being performed on a project, on a task, or by a resource. Conversely, nonworking time is when labor is not being performed. You can modify working time by selecting the **Project** tab on the ribbon, and then selecting the **Change Working Time** button in the **Properties** command group. The *Change Working Time dialog box* enables you to make changes to the selected base calendar.

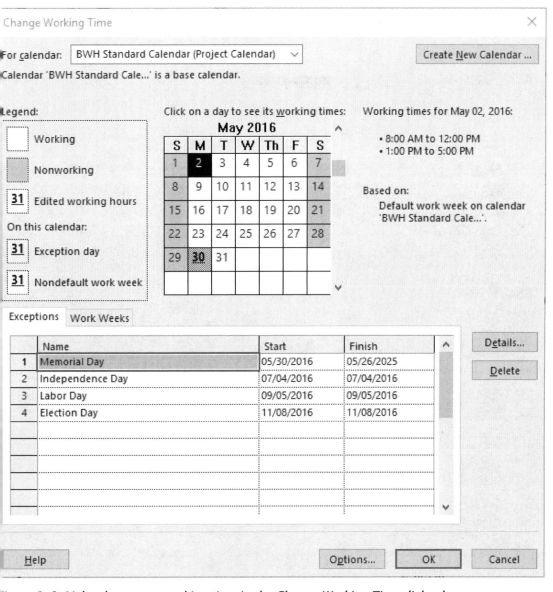

Figure 2-9: Make changes to working time in the Change Working Time dialog box.

The **Change Working Time** dialog box displays a miniature calendar of the project's base calendar. The **Legend** to the left of the miniature calendar briefly explains the coding used on the miniature calendar. The following table expands on the **Legend.**

Item	Meaning
Working Working	Labor is being performed on this date.
Nonworking Nonworking	Labor is not being performed on this date. Weekends and holidays are typically nonworking dates.

Item	Meaning
Edited working hours **31** Edited working hours	The period of time when labor is being performed on this date is different than a normal working day.
Exception day **31** Exception day	Working hours on this date are different than usual. For example, an organization might only be open during the morning on the day before a major holiday.
Nondefault work week **31** Nondefault work week	Working hours during this entire week are different than usual. For example, an organization might be completely shut down for a week.

Exceptions

In Microsoft Project 2016, an *exception* is a day or week when working time is different than what is normal for the base calendar. All exceptions to the base calendar are displayed in a table at the bottom of the **Change Working Time** dialog box.

	Name	Start	Finish
	Exceptions Work Weeks		
1	Memorial Day	05/30/2016	05/26/2025
2	Independence Day	07/04/2016	07/04/2016
3	Labor Day	09/05/2016	09/05/2016
4	Election Day	11/08/2016	11/08/2016
5	Thanksgiving Day	11/24/2016	11/24/2016
6	Black Friday	11/25/2016	11/25/2016
7	Christmas Day (observed)	12/26/2016	12/26/2016
8	New Year's Day (observed)	01/02/2017	01/02/2017

Figure 2-10: An exception to the base calendar might occur for a holiday.

You can add an exception to the base calendar by selecting a date or dates on the miniature calendar in the **Change Working Time** dialog box and entering a name for the exception in the **Exception** table. For example, if your organization is closed for the Thanksgiving holiday, you would select the fourth Thursday of November in the miniature calendar and enter *Thanksgiving* in the highlighted cell of the **Exceptions** table.

Note: Microsoft Office 2016 also enables you to change the normal work week for a base calendar using the **Work Weeks** tab in the **Change Working Time** dialog box. For example, you can change the work week from the default of Monday–Friday to Tuesday–Saturday. This is an advanced skill that is not covered in this course. For more information, type *Change working days for the project calendar* in the **Tell Me** bar field.

Note: To further explore work-week customization, you can access the LearnTO **Change the Work Week** presentation from the **LearnTO** tile on the CHOICE Course screen.

Working Time vs. Non-Working Time

By default, whenever you add an exception to the base calendar, Microsoft Project 2016 assumes that the entire day is nonworking time. However, let's say your organization will only be open from 8:00 A.M. to 12:00 P.M. on Christmas Eve. You can make some of the day working time and some of the day nonworking time by selecting the exception in the **Exceptions** table and then selecting **Details.**

The Details Dialog Box

The **Details** dialog box sets the working times for the selected exception. You can use exceptions to increase normal working hours as well as decrease them. For example, your organization might be open late one night for inventory.

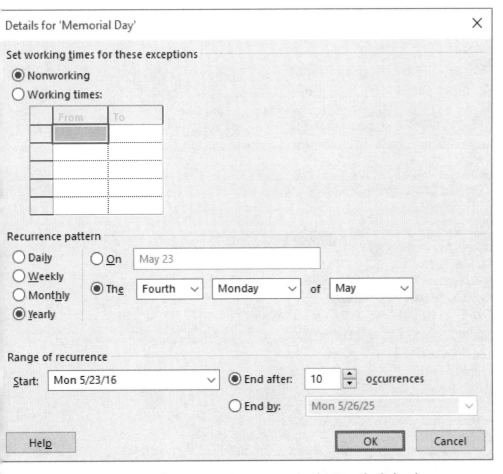

Figure 2-11: Working times for an exception appear in the Details dialog box.

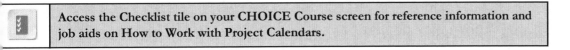

Access the Checklist tile on your **CHOICE** Course screen for reference information and job aids on **How to Work with Project Calendars.**

ACTIVITY 2–3
Creating and Assigning a New Calendar

Before You Begin

The **My_Woods_3BR_Home_Project.mpp** project plan file is open.

Scenario

Building with Heart observes several federal holidays where no project work will be scheduled. Also work is only scheduled for half a day on Election Day. You decide to add these holidays to a new base calendar, and then assign that as the project calendar to make the schedule more accurate.

1. Create a copy of the **Standard** calendar.
   a) On the ribbon, select **Project→Change Working Time**.
   b) In the **Change Working Time** dialog box, select **Create New Calendar**.
   c) In the **Create New Base Calendar** dialog box, in the **Name** field, enter *BWH Standard Calendar*
   d) In the **Make a copy of** field, select **Standard Calendar**.
   e) Select **OK**.
      Verify that the **Change Working Time** dialog box is open and that the **For calendar** field is set to **BWH Standard Calendar**.

2. Add federal holidays as exceptions.
   a) Navigate the calendar to May 2016.
   b) Select **Monday, May 30, 2016**.
   c) In the **Exceptions** table, in the **Name** column, select the highlighted cell.
   d) Type *Memorial Day* and press **Enter**.
   e) Add the following exceptions to the project calendar:
      • Monday, July 4, 2016, Independence Day
      • Monday, September 5, 2016, Labor Day
      • Tuesday, November 8, 2016, Election Day

3. Change the working time of Election Day.
   a) In the **Exceptions** table, select **Election Day**.
   b) Select **Details**.
   c) In the **Details for 'Election Day'** dialog box, select the **Working times** radio button.
   d) Select the second row of the **Working times** table (1:00 PM-5:00 PM).
   e) Press **Delete** to remove the second row.
   f) Select **OK** to close the **Details for 'Election Day'** dialog box.

4. Set a recurrence pattern.
   a) In the **Exceptions** table, select **Memorial Day**.
   b) Select **Details**.
   c) In the **Details for 'Memorial Day'** dialog box, in the **Recurrence pattern** section, select the **Yearly** radio button.
   d) Select the **The Last Monday of May** radio button.
   e) Select the **End after** radio button.
   f) Change the number of occurrences from **1** to **10**.
   g) Select **OK** to close the **Details for 'Memorial Day'** dialog box.

h) Select **OK** to close the **Change Working Time** dialog box.

. Assign **BWH Standard Calendar** as the project calendar.

a) Select **Project→Project Information**.

b) In the **Project Information for 'My_Woods_3BR_Home_Project'**, in the **Calendar** drop-down list, select **BWH Standard Calendar**.

c) Select **OK**.

. Save your changes to **My_Woods_3BR_Home_Project.mpp** and close it.

a) On the ribbon, select **File→Save**.

b) On the ribbon, select **File→Close**.

Summary

In this lesson, you created a new project from a template and set the project's start date. You captured relevant information in the project's properties, and you created a base calendar to reflect your organization's working schedule. By practicing the good habit of properly defining your project plan, you ensure that the plan will be easily understandable and maintainable throughout the life of the project. Over time, you will build a library of solid project plans that you and your organization can draw upon to improve future projects.

Why might you create a new project from a template instead of a blank project plan?

What exceptions to the base calendar will you add to your next project? Will they be recurring?

Note: Check your CHOICE Course screen for opportunities to interact with your classmates, peers, and the larger CHOICE online community about the topics covered in this course or other topics you are interested in. From the Course screen you can also access available resources for a more continuous learning experience.

3 | Creating and Organizing Tasks

Lesson Time: 1 hour, 45 minutes

Lesson Introduction

Now that you've created and defined your project plan, you need to modify the project plan so that it reflects the work that needs to be done for a particular project. You understand that Microsoft® Project Professional 2016 is a very powerful tool for defining and scheduling the details of a project plan, but you may not know just how to do this.

You may already use a task list to keep track of things that need to be done in your personal or professional life. You may use a notepad, or other software tools such as Microsoft Outlook or Excel, to keep track of your tasks. However, when it comes to a robust project plan that can be scheduled to the degree of precision that fits your needs, Project can help you turn a basic task list into a real schedule. In this lesson, you will do just that.

Lesson Objectives

In this lesson, you will create and organize tasks. You will:

- Add tasks to the project plan.

- Import tasks from other programs such as Excel and SharePoint.

- Create and modify a work breakdown structure and milestones.

- Define relationships between tasks and describe task dependencies.

- Schedule tasks and manage constraints and deadlines.

TOPIC A

Add Tasks to a Project Plan

Once you have a Microsoft Project Professional 2016 file, you must update it with detailed information about your project. In this topic, you will enter the tasks that must be performed to complete the project, estimate how much time is needed to perform each task, and link the tasks together into a chain.

Project Tasks

A *task* is a specific chunk of project work. In other words, tasks are the building blocks of effort that need to be done to execute the project. In Microsoft Project Professional 2016, you can use tasks to break a project into manageable pieces of work. You can schedule the duration and sequence of tasks in Project, and assign resources (people or materials) who will perform the tasks.

Figure 3–1: Project tasks are the building blocks of a project plan.

The Task Entry Table

You are already familiar with the **Gantt Chart** view. This view contains the *Task Entry table*, which is the main area in Microsoft Project from which to view, enter, and modify tasks. The **Task Entry** table works very much like other table-based screens. If you have worked with tables in Excel or other programs, you will find similar functionality in Microsoft Project.

ⓘ	Task Mode ▾	Task Name ▾	Duration ▾	Start ▾	Finish ▾	Predecessors
1	⭢	◢ General Conditions	20 days	Mon 5/2/16	Mon 5/30/16	
2	⭢	Finalize plans and develop estimate with owner, architect	20 days	Mon 5/2/16	Fri 5/27/16	
3	⭢	Sign contract and notice to proceed	1 day	Mon 5/30/16	Mon 5/30/16	2
4	⭢	◢ Apply for Permits	0 days	Mon 5/30/16	Mon 5/30/16	
5	⭢	Secure foundation permit	0 days	Mon 5/30/16	Mon 5/30/16	3
6	⭢	Secure framing permit	0 days	Mon 5/30/16	Mon 5/30/16	3

Figure 3-2: You will build the basic structure of your project plan in the Task Entry table.

In the left pane of the **Gantt Chart** view, you will see the **Task Entry** table, which contains the following project information in columns from left to right.

Column	Description
Row Number	The row in the Gantt chart. This number corresponds to the **Task ID** of the task in that row.
Indicators	Little icons that show the status of the tasks, help, and error information. For example, if a task contains a note, this column will show a note indicator.
Task Mode	Shows whether the task is manually or auto scheduled.
Task Name	A brief description of the work. Short, action-oriented task names are best (for example, "Design logo").
Duration	How long the task will take. By default, Microsoft Project 2016 uses days as the unit of time for durations. However, if you wish, you can specify minutes, hours, weeks, or months as the unit of time.
Start	The date when the task is planned to begin.
Finish	The date when the task is planned to be completed.
Predecessors	The **Task ID(s)** of tasks on which this task is dependent to complete.

The Task Information Dialog Box

In the **Gantt Chart** view, whenever you open a task, the *Task Information dialog box* opens. This dialog box contains all the information about the task, grouped into six tabs. The **General** tab displays the task's **Name, Duration, Schedule Mode, Start Date,** and **Finish Date**—which correspond to several of the columns in the **Task Entry** table.

Figure 3-3: Update task data in the Task Information dialog box.

General Task Information

The **General** tab of the **Task Information** dialog box contains much of the same information as the columns in the **Task Entry** table. You can modify the values directly in the table or in the dialog box.

 Note: After you make a change to a task, the changes to the schedule will be highlighted in light blue in the **Gantt Chart** view.

Task Durations

The *Duration* field shows the amount of time it will take to complete the task. Usually, you will know how long it will take to perform a task. However, if you're not sure how long a task will take, you can mark the duration as **Estimated.** If you mark a duration as **Estimated,** it will be shown with a question mark. Conversely, if you type a question mark after a duration, it will be marked as **Estimated.**

Duration: 10d? ▲▼ ☑ Estimated

Figure 3-4: You can enter an estimated Duration if you're not sure how long a task will take.

 Note: If you are using **New Tasks Auto Scheduled** mode, all new tasks will automatically be given an estimated duration of 1 day.

Task Links

When you *link* two tasks together in Microsoft Project 2016, you are creating a *dependency* between their start and finish dates. Dependencies drive the project schedule. A task's *predecessor* re the tasks which drive its schedule, while its *successors* are the tasks which are dependent upon . Every change you make to a linked task will affect its successors, and its successors' successors, nd so on.

y default, whenever you link two tasks in Microsoft Project Professional 2016, a simple *Finish-to-tart (FS)* dependency is established between them. This means that the first task must be ompleted before the second task can begin. The links between tasks are indicated with arrows. If our project is simple, you might link all of the tasks together into a single chain (better known to roject managers as a path). However, in more complex projects, tasks are often linked together to orm multiple paths that may diverge, converge, or run in parallel with one another.

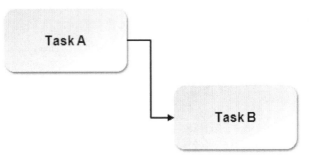

igure 3–5: Linked tasks.

 Note: Other types of dependencies between tasks—*Start-to-Finish (SF)*, *Start-to-Start (SS)*, and *Finish-to-Finish (FF)*—will be discussed later in this course.

ask Selection

ou can select multiple tasks and link them as dependencies using the **Link Selected Tasks** ommand. You can select the first task in a sequence and then use the **Shift** key to select a sequence f tasks, or you can use the **Ctrl** key to select non-contiguous tasks.

 Access the Checklist tile on your CHOICE Course screen for reference information and job aids on How to Add Tasks to a Project Plan.

ACTIVITY 3–1
Adding Tasks to a Project Plan

Data File

C:\091062Data\Creating and Organizing Tasks\Woods_3BR_Home_Project_Tasks.mpp

Scenario

Now that you have a project plan for the Woods family home, you need to add some tasks to it. You know that the clearing of the debris from the lot needs to be completed. You add the tasks that you think will be needed to tear down and clear the old house. You also want to make sure that any reusable materials are either saved for the new home or sent to Building with Heart's recycling center. You need to have some volunteers there to sort the debris and hire multiple trucks to haul the appropriate containers to their different destinations. Since you aren't yet sure how to incorporate these tasks into the overall project plan, you add them at the end of the sheet and will move them later once you learn when those tasks need to be completed.

1. Open the **Woods_3BR_Home_Project_Tasks.mpp** project plan file.
   a) Select **File→Open**.
   b) In the **Open** backstage, select **Browse**.
   c) In the **Open** dialog box, navigate to the **C:\091062Data\Creating and Organizing Tasks** folder containing your class files.
   d) Select **Woods_3BR_Home_Project_Tasks.mpp** and select **Open**.

2. Add a **Demolition of Old House** task.
   a) Make sure that you are in the **Gantt Chart** view.
   b) In the **Task Entry** pane, scroll down to the area where there are empty rows, below row 108.
   c) In the **Task Name** field, type *Demolition of Old House*
   d) In the **Duration** field, type *2 weeks?* to indicate you are estimating the demolition to take two weeks.

3. Add the following tasks below **Demolition of Old House**. If necessary, change the durations to one day.
   - Place Containers
   - Sort Debris
   - Haul Recycling
   - Haul Waste

4. Link the demotion tasks together.
   a) Select all of the tasks you just entered. Be sure to select the first task, **Demolition of Old House**, first and hold down the **Ctrl** key while selecting the following tasks.
   b) On the ribbon, select **Task→Schedule→Link the Selected Tasks**.
      Verify that the tasks are linked in sequence by examining the **Predecessors** column for the tasks.

5. Save your changes as **My_Woods_3BR_Home_Project_Tasks.mpp**.
   a) On the ribbon, select **File→Save As**.
   b) Select **Browse** and then navigate to C:\091062Data\Creating and Organizing Tasks\.
   c) In the **File name** field, enter *My_Woods_3BR_Home_Project_Tasks* and then select **Save**.

TOPIC B

Import Tasks From Other Programs

You have already manually added tasks to a project plan. However, there may be times when a list of tasks has already been created in another program. This is especially true when you are collaborating with others who aren't using Microsoft Project. In this topic, you will import tasks from other programs into your project plan.

Methods of Importing Tasks

 Note: To further explore working with SharePoint, you can access the LearnTO **Sync Project with SharePoint** presentation from the **LearnTO** tile on the CHOICE Course screen.

If you have an existing list of tasks in another program, you can import them into Microsoft Project. Because the **Task Entry** table is just like a spreadsheet, the simplest way to import tasks is to copy them to the clipboard and then paste them into the project plan. You can also create a new project plan from an existing **SharePoint** task list. Project also imports tasks from the following types of files:

File Type	Description
Microsoft Excel	This format, used by the Microsoft Excel spreadsheet program, uses the .xlsx, .xlsb, and .xls extensions.
Text-only or ASCII	Text-only or ASCII format is a generic text format used by word-processing and other programs. This format uses the .txt extension and is tab delimited.
Comma-separated values (CSV)	Comma-separated values (CSV) is a generic text format used with word-processing and other programs. This format uses the .csv extension and is comma delimited, where values are separated by the system list separator, usually a comma or semicolon.
Extensible Markup Language (XML)	Extensible Markup Language (XML) is a format used to deliver rich, structured data in a standard, consistent way. This format uses the .xml extension. Like the MPX format used in older versions of Project, the XML format can be used to interchange project data between Project and other programs.

The Trust Center

By default, Microsoft Project 2016 will not open file formats other than the native project plan format (.mpp and .mpt files). To import data from other file formats, you must first enable the ability to open other file formats in the *Trust Center*. You can access the **Trust Center** from the **Options** dialog box.

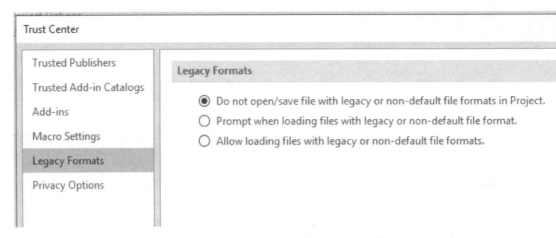

Figure 3–6: Project won't open non-project files unless you enable it to in the Legacy Formats dialog box.

The Import Wizard Dialog Box

When you open a non-project plan file in one of the supported formats, Project will automatically start the *Import Wizard*. The **Import Wizard** walks you though the steps needed to import data from the file.

When you import data from another file type, you need to create an *import map*. This map defines how data from the source file corresponds to data in the project file. For example, if an Excel worksheet has three fields labeled Task Name, Start Date, and Duration, you need to map those fields to corresponding fields in Project to ensure that the data is structured as intended. You can use an existing map, or create a new map.

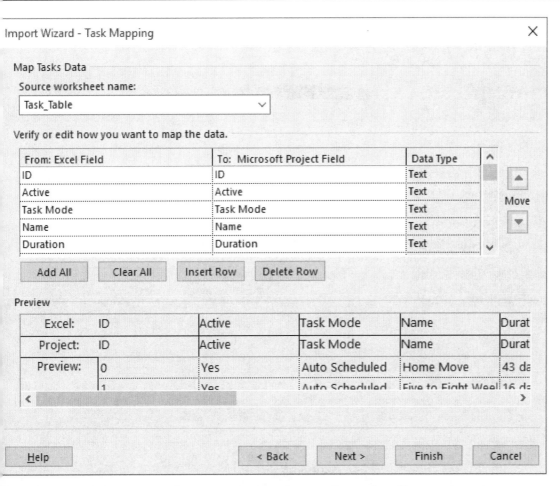

Figure 3-7: The Import Wizard lets you map the columns of your data file to project plan columns.

 Access the Checklist tile on your CHOICE Course screen for reference information and job aids on How to Import Tasks to a Project Plan.

ACTIVITY 3-2
Importing Tasks to a Project Plan

Data Files

C:\091062Data\Creating and Organizing Tasks\Landscape_Task_List.xlsx

C:\091062Data\Creating and Organizing Tasks\Home_move_plan.xlsx

Before You Begin

The **My_Woods_3BR_Home_Project_Tasks.mpp** project plan file is open.

Scenario

Gary Clark is a volunteer at Building with Heart who specializes in environmentally friendly landscaping. He sent you an Excel file that contains some of the tasks that he wants to make sure are included in the project plan for the Woods home. You decide to add his tasks to your plan.

Meanwhile, your new director, Teresa Sanchez, has a file that she thinks was exported from a project management program, maybe even an older version of Project. She says that the file contains the basic tasks that a family needs to follow when moving into a new home. She would like you to try to open it in Microsoft Project and see if it might be something interesting to offer to the Woods and other families as a handout to help them get ready while their home is being built.

---

1. Open the **Landscape_Task_List.xlsx** file in Microsoft Excel.

   a) On the Windows **Taskbar**, select **File Explorer**.

   b) In the **File Explorer** window, navigate to the **C:\091062Data\Creating and Organizing Tasks** folder containing your class files.

   c) Double-click the **Landscape_Task_List.xlsx** file to open it in Excel.

   > **Note:** You do not need to select the **Enable Editing** button since you are not modifying the file.

2. Copy the tasks to the clipboard.

   a) In Excel, select the cells in column **A**, rows **2** through **7**, that contain the task names.

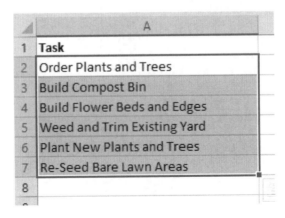

   b) On the **Home** ribbon, select **Copy**.

. Paste the tasks into the **My_Woods_3BR_Home_Project_Tasks.mpp** project plan.

   a) On the **Taskbar**, select the **Project** shortcut to switch back to Microsoft Project.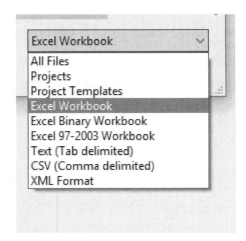
   b) In the **Task Entry** table, scroll down to the empty area.
   c) Place the cursor in the **Task Name** column of the first empty row.
   d) From the **Task** ribbon, select **Paste**.
      Verify that the new tasks appear in the **Task Entry** table.

🔚	Order Plants and Trees	1 day?	Mon 5/2/16	Mon 5/2/16
🔚	Build Compost Bin	1 day?	Mon 5/2/16	Mon 5/2/16
🔚	Build Flower Beds	1 day?	Mon 5/2/16	Mon 5/2/16
🔚	Weed and Trim Ex	1 day?	Mon 5/2/16	Mon 5/2/16
🔚	Plant New Plants a	1 day?	Mon 5/2/16	Mon 5/2/16
🔚	Re-Seed Bare Lawn	1 day?	Mon 5/2/16	Mon 5/2/16

. Save your changes to **My_Woods_3BR_Home_Project_Tasks.mpp** and then close the Project file and the Excel file.

   a) Select **File→Save**.
   b) Select **File→Close** to close **My_Woods_3BR_Home_Project_Tasks.mpp**.
   c) On the Windows **Taskbar**, select **Excel** to switch back to Excel.
   d) On the top-right corner of the Excel window, select **Close** to close Excel. If prompted to save changes, select **No**.

. Import **Home_move_plan.xlsx** as a new project plan.

   a) If necessary, on the Windows **Taskbar**, select **Project** to switch back to Microsoft Project 2016.
   b) Select **File→New**.
   c) In the **New** backstage, select **New from Excel workbook**.
   d) In the **Open** dialog box, navigate to the **C:\091062Data\Creating and Organizing Tasks** folder containing your class files.
   e) In the **Format** drop-down list, select **Excel Workbook (*.xlsx)**.

Excel Workbook ⌄
All Files
Projects
Project Templates
Excel Workbook
Excel Binary Workbook
Excel 97-2003 Workbook
Text (Tab delimited)
CSV (Comma delimited)
XML Format

   f) Select **Home_move_plan.xlsx**, and then select **Open**.
   g) In the **Import Wizard** dialog box, select **Next**.

h) In the **Import Wizard - Map** dialog box, select the **Use existing map** radio button, and then select **Next**.

i) In the **Import Wizard - Map Selection** dialog box, select **Task "Export Table" map**, and then select **Next**.

j) In the **Import Wizard - Import Mode** dialog box, verify that the **As a new project** radio button is selected, and then select **Next**.

k) In the **Import Wizard - Map Options** dialog box, make sure that the selected check boxes are as follows, and then select **Next**.

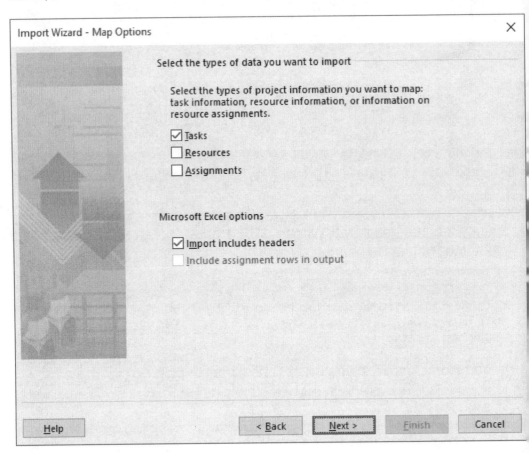

l) In the **Import Wizard - Task Mapping** dialog box, in the **Source worksheet name** list, select **Task_Table** and then select **Finish**.

m) In the message box regarding an error in column 10, select **No**.

n) In the **Microsoft Project** warning dialog box about the start date, select **OK**.

o) Verify that the new project plan is created.

6. Save the new project plan as **My_Family_Home_Move_Plan.mpp** and then close the file.

a) Select **File→Save As**.

b) On the **Save As** backstage, select **Browse** and browse to the **Creating and Organizing Tasks** folder.

c) In the **Save As** dialog box, in the **File Name** field, enter *My_Family_Home_Move_Plan*

d) Select **Save**.

e) Select **File→Close**.

TOPIC C

Create a Work Breakdown Structure

Now that you've added tasks to a project plan, you need a way to group and organize those tasks. In this topic, you will create and modify a work breakdown structure and milestones.

Work Breakdown Structure

The *Work Breakdown Structure (WBS)* is the hierarchical arrangement of the task list. Creating a WBS from your task list helps you organize your tasks and breaks down large tasks into smaller tasks.

The WBS should detail the full scope of work needed to complete the project. This breakdown is essential for estimating project cost, assigning resources, and effective scheduling. Project progress will be based on comparisons between the actual work and the plan as detailed in the WBS. It is important to hone your task list into a completed WBS during the planning process.

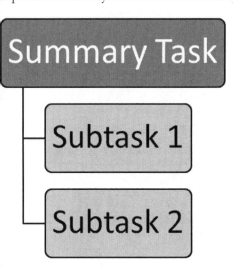

Figure 3-8: You should organize tasks in a hierarchical work breakdown structure.

Summary Tasks and Subtasks

A *summary task* is one that has related *subtasks* grouped below it. In the **Gantt Chart** view, summary tasks are shown with bold text in the left pane and horizontal brackets in the right pane. Subtasks are indented underneath their summary tasks. You can hide some or all of the subtasks underneath a summary task for a high-level view of a project. Summary tasks can also be made into subtasks of a higher summary task, which is helpful if you have complex projects.

◢ **General Conditions**	**21 days**	**Wed 9/9/15**	**Wed 10/7/1!**
Finalize plans and develop estimate with owner, architect	20 days	Wed 9/9/15	Tue 10/6/15
Sign contract and notice to proceed	1 day	Wed 10/7/15	Wed 10/7/15
◢ **Apply for Permits**	**0 days**	**Wed 10/7/15**	**Wed 10/7/15**
Secure foundation permit	0 days	Wed 10/7/15	Wed 10/7/15
Secure framing permit	0 days	Wed 10/7/15	Wed 10/7/15

Figure 3–9: You can collapse and expand summary tasks and subtasks in the Gantt Chart view.

You can create new summary tasks in **Gantt Chart** view using the **Insert Summary Task** button in the **Insert** command group on the **Task** tab of the ribbon. You can convert a regular task into a summary task using the **Outdent Task** button in the **Schedule** command group on the **Task** tab. Conversely, you can convert a regular task into a subtask using the **Indent Task** button in the **Schedule** command group on the **Task** tab.

Grouping tasks under a summary task does not automatically create dependencies among the subtasks. You must link subtasks manually (if they aren't already linked).

You can change the duration of summary tasks, but doing so will not always change the duration of the subtasks. It's better to change the duration of the subtasks, which will change the duration of the summary task.

Two Approaches to Summary Tasks

Sometimes you will create a comprehensive list of project tasks and then group them into summary tasks (the bottom-up approach). Other times you will create a list of high-level tasks that become summary tasks as you add lower-level subtasks below each one (the top-down approach). Neither approach is necessarily better than the other. The bottom-up approach works well when you already have a good idea what needs to happen to complete the project. The top-down approach works best if you only have a general idea of how the project will unfold.

The Project Summary Task

Every new project automatically contains a project summary task. All new tasks you add to a project will be subtasks of the project summary task. Project 2016 hides the project summary task by default in new projects. In **Gantt Chart** view, you can unhide it by selecting the **Format** contextual tab in the ribbon, finding the **Show/Hide** group, and checking the **Project Summary Task** check box. The project summary task will appear as the first task in the Gantt chart and is helpful as it contains the summary, or roll-up, of the overall project plan.

ⓘ	Task Mode ▾	Task Name ▾	Duration ▾	Start ▾	Finish ▾
0	⬛	◢ **Residential Construction**	**152 days**	**Wed 9/9/15**	**Thu 4/7/16**
1	⬛	◢ **General Conditions**	**21 days**	Wed 9/9/15	Wed 10/7/1!
2	⬛	Finalize plans and develop estimate with owner, architect	20 days	Wed 9/9/15	Tue 10/6/15
3	⬛	[Project Summary Task "Task 0"] ...act and notice ...d	1 day	Wed 10/7/15	Wed 10/7/15

Figure 3-10: The project summary task is the highest level task in the work breakdown structure.

Note: The project summary task is sometimes referred to as "Task 0."

Outline Numbers

When you are working with complex projects that have a number of summary tasks and subtasks, you may find it helpful to see the outline numbers that Project 2016 automatically assigns to each task. Project uses a decimal outline numbering scheme to show the sequencing and level of tasks. Project hides the outline number by default. In **Gantt Chart** view, you can unhide the outline numbers by selecting the **Format** contextual tab in the ribbon, finding the **Show/Hide** group, and checking the **Outline Number** check box. The outline numbers will appear before each task in the Gantt Chart.

◢ **1 General Conditions**	**21 days**	**Wed 9/9/15**
1.1 Finalize plans and develop estimate with owner, architect	20 days	Wed 9/9/15
1.2 Sign contract and notice to proceed	1 day	Wed 10/7/15
◢ **1.3 Apply for Permits**	**0 days**	**Wed 10/7/15**
1.3.1 Secure foundation permit	0 days	Wed 10/7/15
1.3.2 Secure framing permit	0 days	Wed 10/7/15
1.3.3 Secure electrical permit	0 days	Wed 10/7/15

Figure 3-11: Outline numbers help you refer to tasks and levels using a numbering system.

Milestone Tasks

A *milestone* is a significant point in the life of your project—such as a deliverable or the end of a phase. In traditional project management practice, milestones are not tasks, do not take time, and do not require resources. However, in Microsoft Project Professional 2016, milestones are tasks that usually have zero duration but may have duration if needed.

| 10.5 Finish Project Milestone | 0 days | Wed | ◆ 9/9 |

Figure 3-12: A project milestone is marked by a diamond on the Gantt chart.

In **Gantt Chart** view, milestones are indicated with a diamond. You can create a new milestone using the **Insert Milestone** button in the **Insert** command group on the **Task** tab of the ribbon. New milestones have zero duration. If you enter a new task in the **Task Entry** table and set the **Duration** column to *0*, Project will automatically convert it to a milestone. You can convert a regular task into a milestone by checking the **Mark task as milestone** check box on the **Advanced** tab of the **Task Information** dialog box. Regular tasks converted to milestones retain their durations and their resources.

Task Notes

You can use the **Notes** tab of the **Task Information** dialog box to add other facts about a task.

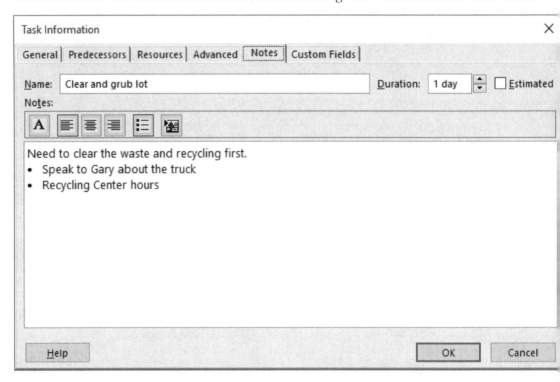

Figure 3-13: You can enter text into the Notes tab of the Task Information dialog box.

There are three methods for adding notes.

Method	Description
Type	You can type text directly into the **Notes** field. You can then format the text using the buttons shown above the field or common keyboard shortcuts (such as **Ctrl +B** for bold, **Ctrl+I** for italics, and **Ctrl+U** for underline).
Copy and paste	You can copy text or graphics from a source document (such as Microsoft® Word, Excel®, or PowerPoint®) and paste them into the **Notes** field. Formatting from the source document is generally retained by the **Notes** field.

Method	Description
Insert object	You can import a file into the **Notes** field by selecting the **Insert Object** button. Almost any Microsoft® Windows® file can be inserted. You have several options for insertion: You can choose to insert a new file or an existing file. If you are inserting an existing file, you can choose to insert a copy of the original file or link to the original file. Finally, you can choose to display the file's contents or an icon of the file.

 Access the Checklist tile on your CHOICE Course screen for reference information and job aids on How to Create a Work Breakdown Structure.

ACTIVITY 3–3
Creating a Work Breakdown Structure

Before You Begin
Project 2016 is open.

Scenario
You added some tasks for clearing the debris of the old home and you imported some tasks for landscaping to the Woods project plan that were provided by the landscaper, Gary Clark. You need to incorporate these tasks into the overall project plan and organize them into the work breakdown structure.

---

1. Rearrange the Task list.

   a) Select **File→Open**.

   b) In the **Open** backstage, select **Recent**, and then select **My_Woods_3BR_Home_Project_Tasks**. Verify that the **My_Woods_3BR_Home_Project_Tasks** opens in Project.

   c) Locate and select the following tasks:

   - 109 - Demolition of Old House
   - 110 - Place Containers
   - 111 - Sort Debris
   - 112 - Haul Recycling
   - 113 - Haul Waste

   d) Right-click the **Task ID** column for **Task 109 - Demolition of Old House** and select **Cut**.

   e) Scroll up to the top of the **Task Entry** table.

   f) Right-click the **Task ID** column for **Task 4 - Apply for Permits** and select **Paste**. Verify that **Apply for Permits** is now in the ninth row below **Haul Waste**.

2. Insert a new summary task for **Clear Old Home**.

   a) Select the five tasks as shown below:

4		⇥	Demolition of Old House	2 wks?	Mon 5/2/16	Fri 5/13/16
5		⇥	Place Containers	1 day?	Mon 5/2/16	Mon 5/2/16
6		⇥	Sort Debris	1 day?	Mon 5/2/16	Mon 5/2/16
7		⇥	Haul Recycling	1 day?	Mon 5/2/16	Mon 5/2/16
8		⇥	Haul Waste	1 day?	Mon 5/2/16	Mon 5/2/16
9		⇥	◢ Apply for Permits	0 days	Mon	Mon

   b) Select **Task→Insert Summary Task**. ⌐

   c) In the **Task Entry** table, in the **Task Name** column of the **<New Summary Task>**, change the text to *Clear Old Home*

3. Replace the **Sod and complete plantings** tasks with the new landscape tasks.

   a) Scroll down and select the following tasks:

   - Order Plants and Trees
   - Build Compost Bin

- Build Flower Beds and Edges
- Weed and Trim Existing Yard
- Plant New Plants and Trees
- Re-Seed Bare Lawn Areas

b) Drag and drop the selected tasks below the task **107 - Install backyard fence**

c) Select the tasks **Sod and complete plantings - front yard** and **Sod and complete plantings - backyard** and then press **Delete**.

Add a note to the **Landscaping and Grounds Work** task.

a) Double-click the summary task, **Landscaping and Grounds Work**.

b) In the **Summary Task Information** dialog box, select the **Notes** tab.

c) In the **Notes** field, enter *Additional tasks provided by Gary Clark.*

d) Select **OK** to close the **Summary Task Information** dialog box.
Verify that the **Task Note** icon appears in the **Indicators** column and position the cursor over it to display the note text.

 Note: If the note text is not immediately visible, you might need to save the file first by using the file name noted in step 7.

Display the project summary task.

a) Scroll to the top of the task list so that **Task 1: General Conditions** is visible.

b) In the **Tell Me** bar, type *Summary Task*

c) In the results list, select **Show Project Summary Task**.
Verify that **Task 0: Woods Family 3BR Home** is visible. You may have to scroll up again to see it.

Add a milestone to the project plan.

a) Scroll to the end of the project plan and select the first empty row.

b) On the **Task** ribbon, select **Insert Milestone**.

c) Rename the new milestone *Ready for Move-In*

d) Select the previous task, **Complete punch list items**.

e) Hold **Shift** and select **Ready for Move-In** so that both tasks are selected.

f) Select **Task→Link Selected Tasks** to link the tasks.

g) Select the **Ready for Move-In** task and select **Task→Scroll to Task** to verify that the milestone appears as a diamond on the Gantt chart.

Save your changes to My_Woods_3BR_Home_Project_Tasks.mpp.

a) Select **File→Save**.

TOPIC D

Define Task Relationships

Now that you've organized your tasks into a hierarchy, you can define more complex task relationships. Tasks aren't always just a list of things that need to be done in order. Sometimes, they must be done at the same time or need to have time left between them. In this topic, you will define relationships between tasks and describe task dependencies.

Task Predecessors

The **Predecessors** tab of the **Task Information** dialog box shows the task's predecessors. A *predecessor* is a task that must be started or finished before another task can begin.

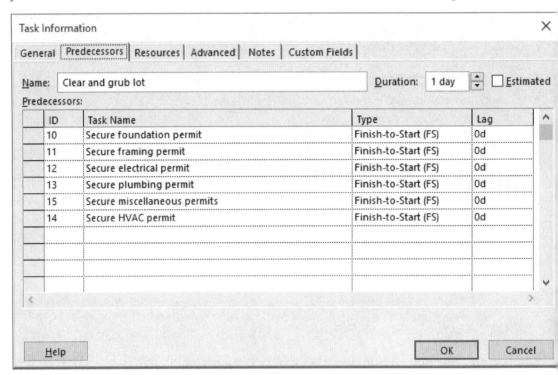

Figure 3-14: You can view a task's predecessors in the Predecessors tab of the Task Information dialog box.

Dependencies

The **Predecessors** tab shows you all of a task's predecessors and their dependencies. A *dependency* is the relationship between a task and its predecessor. The table describes the four types of dependencies.

Dependency	Description	Example
Finish-to-Start (FS) 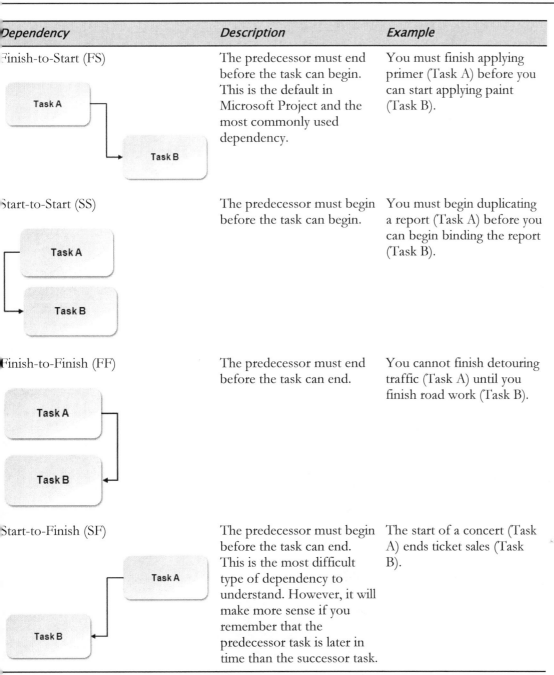	The predecessor must end before the task can begin. This is the default in Microsoft Project and the most commonly used dependency.	You must finish applying primer (Task A) before you can start applying paint (Task B).
Start-to-Start (SS)	The predecessor must begin before the task can begin.	You must begin duplicating a report (Task A) before you can begin binding the report (Task B).
Finish-to-Finish (FF)	The predecessor must end before the task can end.	You cannot finish detouring traffic (Task A) until you finish road work (Task B).
Start-to-Finish (SF)	The predecessor must begin before the task can end. This is the most difficult type of dependency to understand. However, it will make more sense if you remember that the predecessor task is later in time than the successor task.	The start of a concert (Task A) ends ticket sales (Task B).

Lag Time

Normally in a Finish-to-Start (FS) relationship, there is no delay or overlap between the end of Task A and the beginning of Task B.

Figure 3–15: In a normal Finish-to-Start relationship, the second task starts as soon as the first ends.

Lag is a delay in time between two tasks that are linked together. For example, in the following figure, even though Task A and Task B have an FS relationship, Task B is scheduled to begin some time after Task A is completed rather than immediately. You can add lag to a link by opening the **Task Information** dialog box of the successor task, selecting the **Predecessors** tab, and typing a positive value into the **Lag** column.

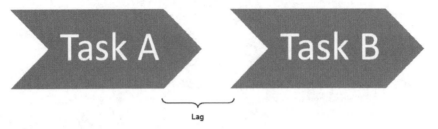

Figure 3-16: Lag is the time between tasks.

Here's a simple example to help you understand lag. Pretend you are making a birthday cake. You must bake the cake before you can put frosting on the cake. So, there is an FS relationship between baking the cake and frosting the cake. However, after you bake the cake, you must wait until the cake has cooled down before you can apply the frosting. The delay period is the lag time.

Lead Time

Lead is an overlap in time between two tasks that are linked together. For example, in the following figure, even though Task A and Task B have an FS relationship, Task B is scheduled to begin when Task A is only about 50 percent complete rather than 100 percent complete. You can add lead to a link by opening the **Task Information** dialog box of the successor task, selecting the **Predecessor** tab, and typing a negative value into the **Lag** column. (In other words, negative lag is lead.)

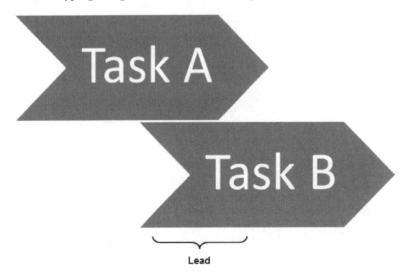

Figure 3-17: Lead time is the overlap in time between dependent tasks.

Here's a simple example to help you understand lead. Let's return to the birthday cake scenario. You must mix the cake's ingredients before you bake the cake in the oven. So, there is an FS relationship between mixing the cake and baking the cake. However, you want the oven to preheat while you are mixing the cake so that the oven will be at the proper temperature for baking when you have finished mixing the cake. The preheating period is the lead time.

 Access the Checklist tile on your CHOICE Course screen for reference information and job aids on How to Define Task Relationships.

ACTIVITY 3-4
Defining Task Relationships

Data File
My_Woods_3BR_Home_Project_Tasks.mpp

Before You Begin
The **My_Woods_3BR_Home_Project_Tasks.mpp** project plan file is open.

Scenario
You have organized your tasks in the project plan and now you want to better define the dependencies between some of the tasks. For example, you know that the **Sort Debris** task cannot finish until the demolition of the old house finishes and it will probably take at least another day for the volunteers to sort through it. You also know that the **Place Containers** task can start as soon as the **Demolition of Old House** task starts, and that the hauling tasks are not necessarily dependent on each other. You have been notified that the demolition crew needs two weeks notice once the contracts are signed before they begin. You make the appropriate changes to the tasks.

1. Create a task relationship with a 2 week lag time.
   a) Double-click the task **5 - Demolition of Old House**.
   b) In the **Task Information** dialog box, select the **Predecessors** tab.
   c) In the **Predecessors** table, in the **ID** column, enter *3*
   d) Move the cursor to the **Task Name** field and verify that it reads **Sign contract and notice to proceed**.
   e) Verify that the **Type** field is set to **Finish-to-Start (FS)**.
   f) In the **Lag** field, enter *2w*.
   g) Click **OK** to close the **Task Information** dialog box.
   h) Verify that the **Predecessors** column for the **Demolition of Old House** task reads **3FS+2 wks**.

2. Create a Start-to-Start relationship between tasks.
   a) Double-click the **6 - Place Containers** task.
   b) On the **Predecessors** tab of the **Task Information** dialog box, verify that the **Demolition of Old House** task is listed in the **Predecessors** table.
   c) In the **Type** column, select **Start-to-Start (SS)**.
   d) Click **OK** to close the **Task Information** dialog box.
   e) Verify that the **Predecessors** column for the **Place Containers** task reads **5SS**.

3. Add a Finish-to-Finish dependency to a task.
   a) Double-click the **7 - Sort Debris** task.
   b) On the **Predecessors** tab of the **Task Information** dialog box, verify that the **Place Containers** task is listed in the **Predecessors** table.
   c) In the first empty row of the **Predecessors** table, in the **ID** column, enter *5*
   d) Move the cursor to the **Task Name** field and verify that it reads **Demolition of Old House**.
   e) In the **Type** column, select **Finish-to-Finish (FF)**.
   f) In the **Lag** field, enter *1d*
   g) Click **OK** to close the **Task Information** dialog box.
   h) Verify that the **Predecessors** column for the **Sort Debris** task reads **6,5FF+1 day**.

4. Change the predecessor of the **Haul Waste** task.

   a) Locate the **Haul Waste** task.

   b) In the **Predecessors** column, replace the current value with the **Task ID** of the **Sort Debris** task, *7.*

5. Save the file as **My_Woods_3BR_Home_Project_Tasks.mpp**.

   a) Select **File→Save**.

TOPIC E

Schedule Tasks

Now that you've defined the relationship between tasks, you can use Microsoft Project to schedule the work. Understanding how Project schedules tasks will help you get the most from your project plans. If you identify the real drivers of tasks in your project, for example that an event has to take place on a certain day, you can use the powerful features of Project to make sure that all the interdependent tasks are scheduled most efficiently. In this topic, you will schedule tasks and manage constraints and deadlines.

Manually Scheduled vs. Auto Scheduled Tasks

Microsoft Project Professional 2016 gives you two options for scheduling tasks: manual and auto. By default, all new tasks you enter in an empty project will be *manually scheduled*. This option gives you complete control over each task's start date, end date, and duration. However, you can choose for new tasks to be *auto scheduled* by Microsoft Project Professional 2016. If you choose this option, the start date, end date, and duration of each task will be automatically determined by the program based on the task's relationship to other tasks, the calendar, and other factors.

Manual scheduling is most useful when your project is just getting started or is simple. However, as your project plan grows and becomes more complex, you will probably want to switch to auto scheduling. Microsoft Project Professional 2016 enables you to switch modes whenever you wish for individual tasks or for all tasks in the project. In some cases, you will want to have some tasks auto scheduled and other tasks manually scheduled.

You can select the **New Tasks** button on the status bar to change whether new tasks are manually or auto scheduled. Use the buttons on the **Task** tab of the ribbon to change whether existing tasks are manually or auto scheduled.

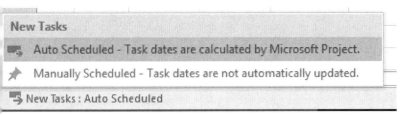

Figure 3-18: You can easily switch between manually scheduled and auto scheduled tasks.

Task Constraints

A *task constraint* is a date-based limitation imposed on a task. You can set task constraints to control the start and finish dates of a task. Tasks can have one of eight schedule constraint types:

* **As Soon As Possible** (the default when projects are scheduled from a start date)
* **As Late As Possible** (the default when projects are scheduled from a finish date)
* **Finish No Earlier Than**
* **Finish No Later Than**
* **Must Finish On**
* **Must Start On**
* **Start No Earlier Than**
* **Start No Later Than**

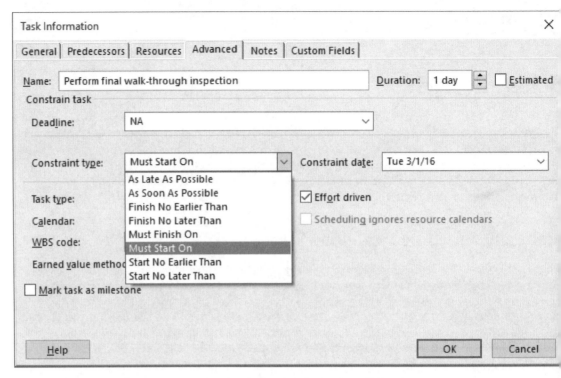

Figure 3-19: Constraint types are set in the Task Information dialog box.

Generally, you should keep the default constraint so that project scheduling remains as flexible as possible. However, you may want to change the constraint if you have a task with a specific date that is critical for project success.

Deadlines

You may be familiar with the concept of deadlines in a variety of contexts, but in Microsoft Project 2016, you can set a *deadline* on a task for the purpose of tracking how close the task finish is to the deadline date. Setting a deadline on a task does not affect the automatic scheduling of a task. It simply gives you a visual indicator that you can use to monitor progress.

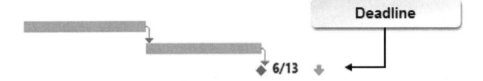

Figure 3-20: A green arrow marks the deadline date in the Gantt chart.

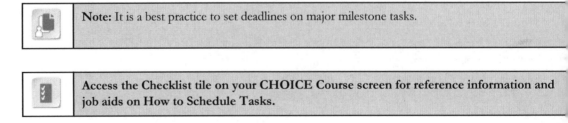

Note: It is a best practice to set deadlines on major milestone tasks.

Access the Checklist tile on your CHOICE Course screen for reference information and job aids on How to Schedule Tasks.

ACTIVITY 3-5
Scheduling Tasks

Data File

My_Woods_3BR_Home_Project_Tasks.mpp

Before You Begin

The **My_Woods_3BR_Home_Project_Tasks.mpp** file is open.

Scenario

You have continued to create the appropriate relationships in your work breakdown structure and now you have some new information that you need to reflect in the project schedule. You have been informed that the recycling center is scheduled to move to a larger facility and that they will not be accepting any recycling during June 2016. The earliest they will be accepting recycling is July 5th, 2016. Also, your director is adamant that the project is completed before the end of the calendar year so that the budget does not have to carry over. You make these schedule adjustments to the project plan.

---

1. Set a constraint on the **Haul Recycling** task.
   a) Double-click the **8 - Haul Recycling** task.
   b) In the **Task Information** dialog box, select the **Advanced** tab.
   c) In the **Constraint type** drop-down list, select **Start No Earlier Than**.
   d) In the **Constraint date** date box, select **July 5, 2016**.
   e) Select **OK** to close the **Task Information** dialog box.

   f) Verify that the **Constraint** icon appears in the **Indicators** column.

2. Add a deadline to the last task.
   a) Scroll down and locate the last task, the **120 - Ready for Move-In** milestone, and double-click it.
   b) In the **Task Information** dialog box, select the **Advanced** tab.
   c) In the **Deadline** date box, select **December 31, 2016**.
   d) Select **OK** to close the **Task Information** dialog box.

   e) Verify that the **Deadline** marker appears in the Gantt chart.

3. Save your changes to **My_Woods_3BR_Home_Project_Tasks.mpp** and close the file.
   a) Select **File→Save**.
   b) Select **File→Close**.

Summary

In this lesson, you added and organized tasks and created relationships in your project plan. Creating a robust, well-thought-out work breakdown structure is an important part of project management. By identifying the tasks that have special relationship and dependency requirements, you will be ready to manage your resources and handle any scheduling issues that come up during project execution. Taking advantage of these features while leaving your project plan flexible enough to adapt to change will save you effort down the road.

Besides the Finish-to-Start dependency, which of the other dependency types (Start-to-Start, Finish-to-Finish, Start-to-Finish) might you use and why?

Which of the task scheduling features do you think will have the greatest impact on your future project plans?

 Note: Check your CHOICE Course screen for opportunities to interact with your classmates, peers, and the larger CHOICE online community about the topics covered in this course or other topics you are interested in. From the Course screen you can also access available resources for a more continuous learning experience.

4 | Managing Project Plan Resources

Lesson Time: 1 hour, 15 minutes

Lesson Introduction

Now that you have created a work breakdown structure, you must define who and what is needed to complete the project tasks. As a project manager, one of the main areas you need to focus on during the planning phase of a project is resources. You have to determine the people, tools, equipment, and materials that will be required for the project. Defining resource requirements early will solidify your project plan and help you adjust as resource availability changes over the life of the project.

Lesson Objectives

In this lesson, you will manage project plan resources. You will:

- Add resources to a project and assign them to tasks.

- Create a calendar for a resource.

- Enter costs for different types of resources.

- Assign resources to tasks.

- Resolve resource conflicts in a project plan.

TOPIC A

Add Resources to a Project Plan

Once you have entered project tasks into a blank Microsoft® Project Professional 2016 file, project resources are the next critical set of data. In this topic, you will add resources to a project and assign those resources to your project tasks.

Resources

Resources are people, equipment, materials, or other costs that are used to accomplish a project task. In other words, resources are the staff, supplies, equipment, and other expenses that you need to execute a project. In Microsoft Project Professional 2016, you can define your resources and assign them to tasks.

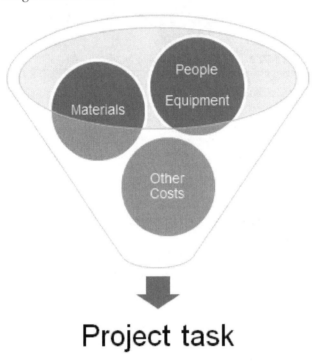

Project task

Figure 4-1: Resources are assigned to project tasks.

Work Resources

A *work resource* is a resource that is employed on a time basis. The most common work resources are the people who will perform the tasks, also known as human resources. You can refer to work resources by name (Gary Clark), or by generic labels (Landscaper) depending on your needs. In addition to human resources, work resources also include resources that you need to schedule or track cost on a time basis. For example, a printing press can only run one job at a time, so you may need to schedule based on its availability. Or, you may need to rent equipment, such as a moving truck, to perform a task and you need to schedule most efficiently to minimize cost. Space can also be treated as a work resource if you need to schedule around its availability or track its cost by time. Examples include conference rooms, storage, convention centers, and so on.

You can also specify the maximum number of units that the resource can work on the project. For example, a person may only be able to devote 50% of his or her time to the project, or, if you have three identical pieces of equipment, you can create one resource for all three and set the **Max Units** field to 300%.

Cost Resources

A *cost resource* is a resource used to capture expenses or track a budget. A *budget resource* is a special type of cost resource used to keep track of costs versus budget through the project lifecycle. Standard cost resources are assigned to tasks to keep track of expenses associated with the task such as a travel expense, purchase of a license, and so on. Budget resources can only be assigned to the project summary task and are used to track the budget at the project level.

Material Resources

A *material resource* is a resource that is measured by how many units are used. For example, you may need to use carpet to complete a flooring task. If you purchase carpet by the square foot, you can create a material resource for the carpet and set its unit of measure to square foot. You can also enter the cost per unit and have Project calculate estimated costs per task.

The Resource Sheet

When you select the **Resource Sheet** button on the **View** bar, the **Resource Sheet** will be displayed. (You may need to scroll down the **View** bar to see the **Resource Sheet** button.) The *Resource Sheet* view shows you all the resources that you have defined for the project. You will see information about the resource in columns.

❶	Resource Name ▼	Type ▼	Material Label ▼	▼	Gr ▼	Max. Units ▼	Std. Rate ▼	Ovt. Rate ▼	Cost/Use ▼	Accrue At ▼	Base Calendar ▼
1	Contractor	Work		C		100%	$50.00/hr	$75.00/hr	$0.00	Prorated	Standard
2	Tools	Cost		T						Prorated	
3	Wood Fence	Material	board	W			$20.00		$0.00	Prorated	

Figure 4-2: You can view and enter resources on the Resource Sheet.

The table describes the first seven columns, from left to right. The other columns will be discussed later in this course.

Column	Description
Row Number	This is simply the row in the resource sheet. This number is not actually part of a resource's information.
Indicators	These are pictures that show the status of the resources. For example, if a resource contains a note, a note indicator will be shown in this column.
Resource Name	This is a brief description of the resource. If the resource is a person, you can use the person's name.
Type	This indicates the kind of resource. In Microsoft Project Professional 2016, the types of resources are **Work, Material,** and **Cost.**
Material Label	This is the unit of measure (pounds, gallons, boxes, and so forth) for material resources.
Initials	This is an abbreviation for the **Resource Name.** For example, Gloria Rodriquez could be abbreviated as GR.
Group	This is usually the department or team to which the resource belongs. For example, Gloria Rodriquez might be part of the Advertising group.

Note: You can paste resource information into the **Resource Sheet** just as you can tasks into the **Task Entry** table. You can also import resources from other programs.

The Resource Information Dialog Box

In the **Resource Sheet** view, whenever you double-click the row number of a resource, the *Resource Information dialog box* opens. This dialog box contains all the information about the resource, grouped into four tabs. Notice that the **General** tab displays the **Resource name, Initials, Group, Type,** and **Material label** fields that correspond to several of the columns in the **Resource Sheet** view. If you provide email addresses for resources, you will be able to send them email from within Project.

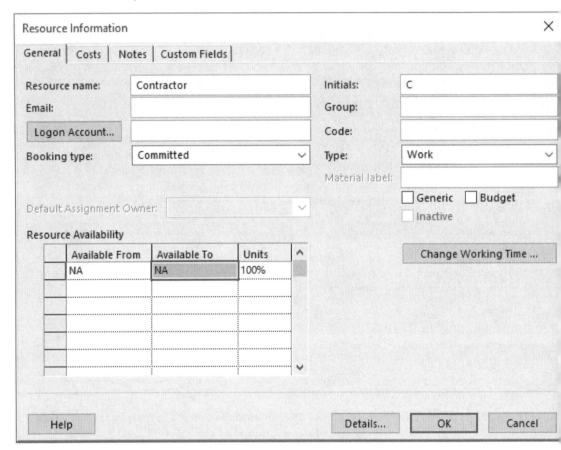

Figure 4–3: The Resource Information dialog box.

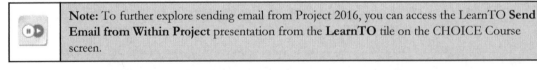 **Note:** To further explore sending email from Project 2016, you can access the LearnTO **Send Email from Within Project** presentation from the **LearnTO** tile on the CHOICE Course screen.

 Access the Checklist tile on your CHOICE Course screen for reference information and job aids on How to Add Resources.

ACTIVITY 4-1
Adding Resources

Data File

C:\91062Data\Managing Project Plan Resources\Woods_3BR_Home_Project_Resources.mpp

Before You Begin

Microsoft Project 2016 is open.

Scenario

You've created a solid work breakdown structure and now it is time to enter the resources that you want to track for your project. The construction company will be handing all of the standard materials once construction starts, but you will be responsible for tracking the volunteer resources, equipment, and materials provided through Building with Heart. You will have four volunteers that can do any kind of work, but you won't know their names until closer to the project start date. You have one volunteer, Gary Clark, who is the landscape expert. You will need to rent at least two containers for the waste and recycling. You will be allowed to use the organization's dump truck for free, but there is a waste dumping fee charged per ton. You also need to create an overall budget for your project and a cost resource for construction estimates. You enter these resources into your project plan.

. Open the **Woods_3BR_Home_Project_Resources.mpp** project plan file.

   a) Select **File→Open**.
   b) In the **Open** backstage, select **Browse**.
   c) In the **Open** dialog box, navigate to the **C:\91062Data\Managing Project Plan Resources** folder containing your class files.
   d) Select **Woods_3BR_Home_Project_Resources.mpp** and select **Open**.

. Add four volunteers to the **Resource Sheet**.

   a) In the **View Bar**, scroll down and select **Resource Sheet**.
   b) In the first empty row of the **Resource Sheet**, in the **Resource Name** column, enter *Volunteer 1* and then press **Enter**.
   c) Repeat for the next three rows to enter *Volunteer 2*, *Volunteer 3*, and *Volunteer 4*

. Change the **Resource Name** of the **Landscape contractor** resource to *Gary Clark*

   a) Locate the resource in row 22, **Landscape contractor**.
   b) In the **Resource Name** field, enter *Gary Clark*

. Add a work resource named **Container**.

   a) In the first empty row of the **Resource Sheet**, in the **Resource Name** column, enter *Container*

. Add a material resource for waste dumping.

   a) In the first empty row of the **Resource Sheet**, in the **Resource Name** column, enter *Waste Dump Fee*
   b) In the **Type** column, choose **Material**.
   c) In the **Material Label** column, enter *ton*

6. Add a cost resource for construction costs.

   a) In the first empty row of the **Resource Sheet**, in the **Resource Name** column, enter *Construction Fixed Cost*

   b) In the **Type** column, select **Cost**.

7. Add a cost resource for the project budget.

   a) In the first empty row of the **Resource Sheet**, in the **Resource Name** column, enter *Project Budget*

   b) In the type column, select **Cost**.

   c) Double-click the **Project Budget** resource.

   d) In the **Resource Information** dialog box, select the **General** tab if necessary, and then select the **Budget** check box.

   e) Select **OK** to close the **Resource Information** dialog box.

8. Save the file as **My_Woods_3BR_Home_Project_Resources.mpp**.

   a) On the ribbon, select **File→Save As**.

   b) Select **Browse** and then navigate to C:\091062Data\Managing Project Plan Resources.

   c) In the **File name** field, enter *My_Woods_3BR_Home_Project_Resources* and select **Save**.

TOPIC B

Create a Resource Calendar

Now that you've entered resources into your project plan, you may also need to create custom calendars for the resources to account for availability of individual people or other work resources. In this topic, you'll do just that.

Resource Calendars

If you have created and applied a base calendar for your project before you start building your resource list, that calendar will automatically appear in the **Base Calendar** column for each work resource. However, if the working and nonworking times of your project calendar do not coincide with the availability of a resource, you can create a *resource calendar*. A resource calendar is specific to a particular resource. For example, a resource calendar might reflect a resource's personal vacation schedule.

If you are using Microsoft Project Professional in an environment with Microsoft SharePoint or Project Server and integrated with your email server, the human resources in your project can update their own calendars. If configured by your administrator, this will enable Project to alert you to any potential conflicts.

Resource Availability

There are times when a resource may not be available until a certain date or not available after a certain date. For example, you may need to hire a contractor who doesn't start until a certain date. Or, you may depend on a person who is moving to another department at the end of the month or a piece of equipment that must be returned by a certain date. In these cases, you can use the *Resource Availability* table in the **Resource Information** dialog box to set a start and/or end date for the resource. You can also use the availability table to set a time period when a resource has more or less availability to work on the project. For example, if a person can only spend half of his or her time working on the project before a certain date, you can set his or her **Units** to 50% during that time period.

Resource Availability

	Available From	Available To	Units	^
	9/21/2015	3/31/2016	100%	
				v

Figure 4–4: The Resource Availability table specifies a start or end date for a resource.

 Access the Checklist tile on your CHOICE Course screen for reference information and job aids on How to Create a Resource Calendar.

ACTIVITY 4–2
Creating a Resource Calendar

Before You Begin
The **My Woods_3BR_Home_Project_Resources.mpp** file is open.

Scenario
You have just received an email from Gary Clark notifying you of his availability for the project. He is going to be assisting with the move of the Recycling Center and taking a vacation the week of July 4th, 2016, so he will not be able to start on the project until July 11, 2016. Also, he volunteers to teach urban gardening on Fridays, so he will only be available Mondays through Thursdays. You create a resource calendar for Gary.

1. Change the resource availability for **Gary Clark**.
   a) Open the **Resource Sheet** if necessary and double-click the resource **Gary Clark**.
   b) Verify that the **General** tab of the **Resource Information** dialog box is displayed.
   c) In the **Resource Availability** table, in the first row in the **Available From** column, select **July 11, 2016** and in the **Available To** column, select **December 31, 2017**.

2. Modify the work week for **Gary Clark**.
   a) On the **General** tab of the **Resource Information** dialog box, select **Change Working Time**.
   b) In the **Base calendar** drop-down list, select **BWH Standard Calendar**.
   c) Select the **Work Weeks** tab.
   d) Verify that the **[Default]** work week is selected, and then select **Details**.
   e) In the **Select days** field, select **Friday**.
   f) Select the **Set days to nonworking time** radio button.
   g) Select **OK** to close the **Details for '[Default]'** dialog box.
   h) Select **OK** to close the **Change Working Time** dialog box.
   i) Select **OK** to close the **Resource Information** dialog box.

3. Save changes to **My_Woods_3BR_Home_Project_Resources.mpp**.
   a) Select **File→Save**.

TOPIC C

Enter Costs for Resources

Now that you've set up your resources and adjusted their availability, you can define how the resources accumulate cost. This will give you further flexibility in tracking your costs as the project progresses.

Resource Costs

The **Cost rate table** on the **Cost** tab enables you to see, add, and change the costs associated with a resource. You can set a resource's normal **Standard Rate, Overtime Rate,** and **Per Use Cost.**

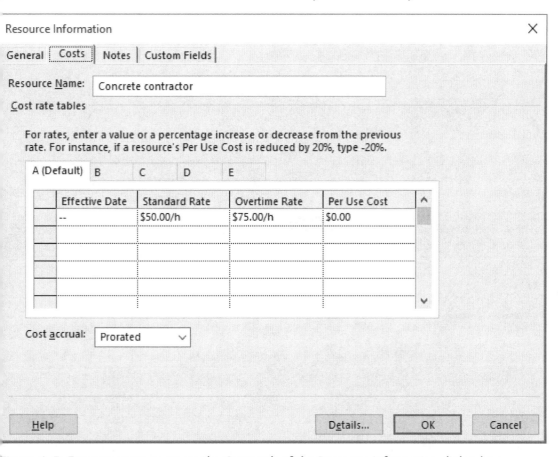

Figure 4-5: Enter resource costs on the Costs tab of the Resource Information dialog box.

You can specify different rates beginning on specified dates. There are two methods for doing this. The first method is to enter the changed rate as a number (such as *110*). The second method is to enter the changed rate as a percentage of the old rate (such as *10%*). When using the second method, you must add the percent sign or Project 2016 will interpret it as a number. Entering a positive percentage increases the rate, and a negative percentage decreases the rate.

Resource Cost Rate Tables

Resources don't always remain at the same rates over the life of a project. People may get raises that take effect on a certain date, or a contractor may charge different rates depending on the type of work being performed. You can specify how costs change using cost tables. The cost tables are lettered. Each table can contain rates that change at specified time periods. For example, you can use **Cost Table A** to specify the default rates of a resource and any change in that resource's default rate, such as a raise, or a discount during the off-season. You can use multiple cost tables if a resource has different rate schedules that may come into play during a project. For example, a contractor may charge more for tasks that are dangerous. You can create a cost table that can be specified at the time you assign the resource to the task to reflect the different rate.

You can also use cost tables with material resources. For example, you may have discounted rates for buying larger quantities or different rates depending on the choice of material quality. You can use the cost rate tables to see how the variable rates affect the project cost when you change them.

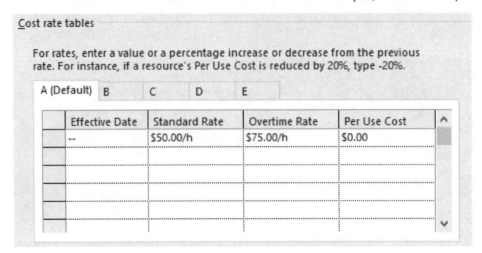

Figure 4–6: Use Cost Rate Tables to record changing rates over the life of a project.

 Access the Checklist tile on your CHOICE Course screen for reference information and job aids on How to Enter Resource Costs.

ACTIVITY 4-3
Entering Resource Costs

Before You Begin

The **My_Woods_3BR_Home_Project_Resources.mpp** project plan file is open.

Scenario

You have some information back on your estimate requests for the Woods family home. The container rental fee is about $20 per day and two are available. The waste dumping fee is about $150 per ton. Also, the maid service is informing you that they are raising their rates from $40 per hour to $50 per hour on 12/15/2016. You capture these resource costs in your project plan.

1. Enter the **Container** rental cost.

   a) If necessary, in the **View Bar**, select **Resource Sheet** to display the **Resource Sheet** view.

   b) In the **Resource Sheet**, locate the **Container** resource.

   c) In the **Max. Units** column, enter *200%*

   d) In the **Std. Rate** column, enter *$20/day*

2. Set the waste dumping fee.

   a) In the **Resource Sheet**, locate the **Waste Dump Fee** resource.

   b) In the **Std. Rate** column, enter *$150*

3. Enter the rate information for the maid service.

   a) In the **Resource Sheet**, double-click the **Maid service** resource.

   b) In the **Resource Information** dialog box, select the **Costs** tab.

   c) In the first row of **Cost Rate Table A**, change the value of the **Standard Rate** column to *$40/h*

   d) In the first empty row of **Cost Rate Table A**, in the **Effective Date** column, select **December 15, 2016.**

   e) In the **Standard Rate** column for the new row, enter *$50/h*

   f) Select **OK** to close the **Resource Information** dialog box.

4. Save your changes to **My_Woods_3BR_Home_Project_Resources.mpp**.

   a) Select **File→Save**.

TOPIC D

Assign Resources to Tasks

After you plan tasks and add resources, you need to make a connection between the tasks and the resources that will be used to complete the tasks. In this topic, you will assign resources to tasks.

The Team Planner View

The *Team Planner* view is the easiest way to see how your resources are allocated across the project. You can find the **Team Planner** view by scrolling down the **View Bar.** Alternatively, you can select the **Resource** tab on the ribbon, and **Team Planner** will be the default displayed in the **View** command group on the far left.

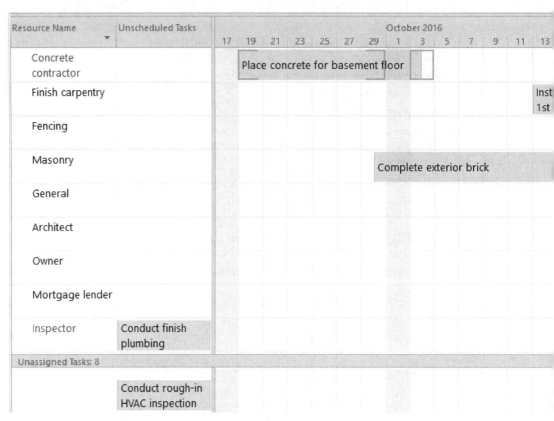

Figure 4–7: Resources in the Team Planner view.

In the **Team Planner** view, all the work resources are shown in the left pane. The tasks to which they are assigned are displayed in the right pane, plotted along the project timeline. Unassigned task appear in the bottom pane of the **Team Planner.** You can assign a task to a single resource by dragging it from the bottom pane to a date in the desired resource's row. Similarly, you can reassign a task by dragging it from one resource's row to another. You can also reschedule a task by dragging it from one date to another.

The Assign Resources Dialog Box

From the **Gantt** chart view, you can use the **Assign Resources** dialog box to assign resources to tasks. While the **Assign Resources** dialog box is open, you can still select tasks in the **Task Entry** table to change which tasks are being assigned quickly. You can use this dialog box to assign a single resource to more than one task. For example, consider the tasks "Draw plans" and "Review blueprints." It makes sense that the architect would be assigned to both of these tasks. You can also assign multiple resources to a single task.

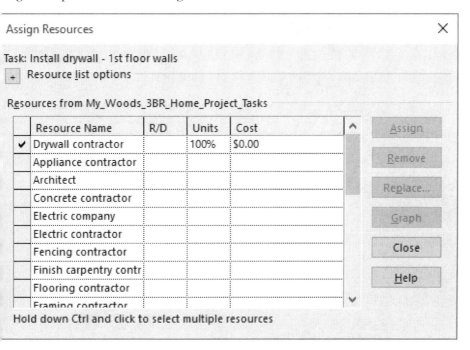

Figure 4-8: The Assign Resources dialog box is where you manage the assignment between resources and tasks.

The Task Usage Table

The *Task Usage table* displays a list of tasks showing assigned resources under each task. Each of the rows under a task represents the link between a particular task and a single resource. The details for the assignments, such as planned work and cost, are displayed in the columns.

	ⓘ	Task Mode ▾	Task Name ▾	Work ▾	Duration ▾	Start ▾	Finish ▾
1		⬛➔	◢ **General Conditions**	**230.4 hrs**	**20 days?**	**Mon 5/2/16**	**Mon 5/30/16**
2		⬛➔	◢ Finalize plans and	198.4 hrs	20 days	Mon 5/2/16	Fri 5/27/16
			General contra	*80 hrs*		*Mon 5/2/16*	*Fri 5/27/16*
			Architect	*80 hrs*		*Mon 5/2/16*	*Fri 5/27/16*
			Owner	*19.2 hrs*		*Mon 5/2/16*	*Fri 5/27/16*
			Mortgage lenc	*19.2 hrs*		*Mon 5/2/16*	*Fri 5/27/16*
3		⬛➔	◢ Sign contract and r	32 hrs	1 day	Mon 5/30/16	Mon 5/30/16
			General contra	*8 hrs*		*Mon 5/30/16*	*Mon 5/30/16*
			Architect	*8 hrs*		*Mon 5/30/16*	*Mon 5/30/16*
			Owner	*8 hrs*		*Mon 5/30/16*	*Mon 5/30/16*
			Mortgage lenc	*8 hrs*		*Mon 5/30/16*	*Mon 5/30/16*
4		⬛➔	Demolition of Old	0 hrs	2 wks?	Mon 5/2/16	Fri 5/13/16

Figure 4-9: View the details for all of a task's assigned resources in the Task Usage table.

The Assignment Information Dialog Box

The *Assignment Information dialog box* provides detailed information about the assignment between a resource and a task. In this dialog box, you can adjust the work hours assigned, adjust the units for work or materials, and set which **Cost Rate** table will be used to calculate the costs for the assignment. You can open the **Assignment Information** dialog box by double-clicking an assignment in the **Task Usage** table.

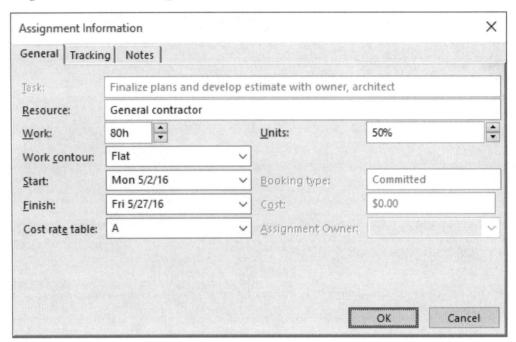

Figure 4–10: View and update details about an assignment in the Assignment Information dialog box.

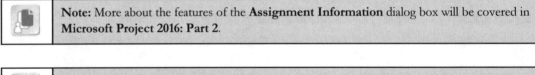

Note: More about the features of the **Assignment Information** dialog box will be covered in **Microsoft Project 2016: Part 2**.

Access the Checklist tile on your CHOICE Course screen for reference information and job aids on How to Assign Resources.

ACTIVITY 4-4
Assigning Resources to Tasks

Before You Begin
The **My_Woods_3BR_Home_Project_Resources.mpp** project plan file is open.

Scenario
Now that you've added some resources and tasks, you need to make assignments. You believe that with four volunteers, you can sort the debris in five working days. Gary Clark will be performing many of the tasks. There should be about 20 tons (2 truckloads) of debris to take to the dump. You've also received the estimate from the construction company of $180,000. Also, your director has set the maximum project budget to $250,000. You make the changes to your project plan. You decide to try **Team Planner** view to quickly make a simple assignment.

1. Assign a resource to **Demolition of Old House** using **Team Planner** view.

   a) On the ribbon, select **Resource→Team Planner** to open **Team Planner** view.

   b) In the **Unassigned Tasks** area, scroll to the **Demolition of Old House** task.

   c) In the **Resource Name** area, scroll to **Site excavation**.

   d) Drag and drop the **Demolition of Old House** task onto the **Site excavation** resource name. The task will automatically drop in the proper place in the schedule.

   e) Verify that the **Demotion of Old House** task is scheduled in the **Site excavation** resource row.

2. Assign volunteers to the **Sort Debris** task.

   a) In the **View** bar, select **Gantt Chart**.

   b) In the **Task Entry** table, locate the **7 - Sort Debris** task.

   c) In the **Resource Names** column, select the drop-down arrow, and then check the boxes for **Volunteer 1**, **Volunteer 2**, **Volunteer 3**, and **Volunteer 4**.

   d) In the **Duration** column, change the value to *5 days*

3. Assign the **Container** resource.

   a) In the **Task Entry** table, select the **Place Containers** task.

   b) On the **Resource** ribbon, select **Assign Resources**.

   c) In the **Assign Resources** dialog box, locate the row for the **Container** resource.

   d) In the **Units** column, enter *200%*

   e) Select **Assign**.

   f) Without closing the **Assign Resources** dialog box, in the **Task Entry** table, select the **Sort Debris** task.

   g) In the **Assign Resources** dialog box, select **Container** and enter *200%* in the **Units** column.

   h) Select **Assign**.

   i) In the **Assign Resources** dialog box, select the **Container** resource.

   j) Drag and drop the **Container** resource to the **Haul Recycling** and **Haul Waste** tasks.

4. Assign multiple tasks to **Gary Clark**.

   a) Without closing the **Assign Resources** dialog box, in the **Task Entry** table, hold the **Ctrl** key while selecting the **Place Containers**, **Haul Recycling**, and **Haul Waste** tasks.

   b) In the **Assign Resources** dialog box, select **Gary Clark**, and then select **Assign**.

5. Assign the **Waste Dump Fee** resource.
   a) In the **Task Entry** pane, select the **Haul Waste** task.
   b) In the **Assign Resources** dialog box, select the **Waste Dump Fee** resource.
   c) In the **Units** column, enter *20*
   d) Select **Assign**.
   e) Verify that the **Units** column reads *20 ton* and the **Cost** column reads *$3,000.00*

6. Assign the **Construction Fixed Cost** resource.
   a) In the **Task Entry** pane, select the **General Conditions** task.
   b) In the **Assign Resources** dialog box, select the **Construction Fixed Cost** resource.
   c) Select **Assign**.

7. Assign the **Project Budget** resource to the project summary task.
   a) On the ribbon, select **Format** and ensure that the **Project Summary Task** check box is checked.
   b) Drag the **Project Budget** resource to the project summary task **Woods Family 3BR Home (Task 0)**.
   c) Select **Close** to close the **Assign Resources** dialog box.

8. Enter the construction estimate and project budget.
   a) On the **View Bar**, select **Task Usage**.
   b) Under **General Conditions**, double-click **Construction Fixed Cost**.
   c) In the **Assignment Information** dialog box, select the **General** tab if necessary.
   d) In the **Cost** field, enter *$180,000*
   e) Select **OK** to close the **Assignment Information** dialog box.
   f) In the **Task Usage** table, select the column header for the first empty column on the right, **Add New Column**, and then select **Budget Cost**.
   g) In the **Project Budget** row, in the **Budget Cost** column, enter *$250,000*

9. Save the changes to **My_Woods_3BR_Home_Project_Resources.mpp** and close the file.
   a) Select **File→Save**.
   b) Select **File→Close**.

TOPIC E

Resolve Resource Conflicts

After you enter resources for your project and assign them to your project, it's a good idea to make sure you aren't planning to give your resources more project work to do than they have time available. When you find that some resources have too much project work assigned to them, you will want to reassign the extra work to other resources that aren't being used to capacity.

Overallocation

Allocation is the scheduling of tasks and resources, taking into account both resource availability and project duration. A resource is *over-allocated* when it is assigned to do more work on a project than it can do within its normal working capacity. For example, if you schedule Samantha Barlow to spend 100% of her time on Task A and 50% of her time on Task B during the same period of time, she is an over-allocated resource.

In the **Gantt** view, tasks with overallocated resources will display an overallocation indicator in the **Indicators** column. The red icon is sometimes referred to as the burning man indicator. In **Team Planner** view, when a work resource is over-allocated, it will be shown in red text in the left pane. The tasks to which the resource is assigned will be shown with red brackets around them in the right pane.

Figure 4-11: Over-allocated resources show in red.

Methods of Resolving Resource Conflicts

When you identify over-allocated work resources, you should level them. *Leveling* is the rescheduling and reassignment of tasks to resolve resource over-allocations.

There are several approaches to leveling:

- Increasing the duration of a task. This approach is used when resources are fixed.
- Increasing the number of resources assigned to a task. This approach is used when task duration is fixed.
- Reassigning a task to another resource who has free time.
- Rescheduling a task.

Project managers typically use a combination of these approaches to achieve a level project.

The Task Inspector Pane

The *Task Inspector* pane displays the critical factors which affect a task's scheduling. If the task has overallocated resources, the **Task Inspector** pane will give you information about the resources and, if available, methods for quickly resolving them. For example, you can have Project move the start date of the task to the next time the resource is available.

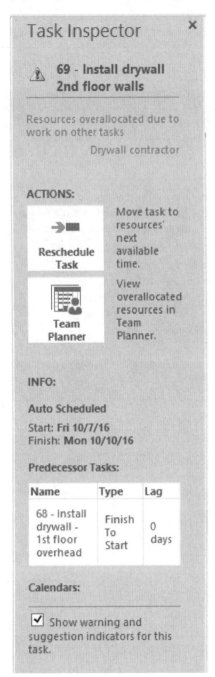

Figure 4–12: The Task Inspector pane gives you information on overallocations and quick resolutions if available.

Automatic Resource Leveling

Microsoft Project 2016 enables you to automatically level over-allocations. Leveling works by splitting tasks or by adding delay to tasks until the resources that are assigned to those tasks are no longer overloaded. Because of these changes to the tasks, leveling can delay the finish date of some tasks and consequently also the project's finish date. When it is leveling, Project does not change who is assigned to each task. Project levels only the work resources, generic resources, and committed resources. It does not level the material resources, cost resources, or proposed resources.

Note: It's a best practice to only allow Project to automatically level over-allocations for specific resources at a time before resorting to **Level All**.

Task Priorities

Prior to leveling, you may want to set the task priorities in the **Task Information** dialog box. The priority sets the task's importance and its availability for leveling. The priority value that you enter is a subjective value between 1 and 1000, which enables you to specify the amount of control you have over the leveling process. For example, if you don't want Project to level a particular task, set its priority level to 1000. By default, priority values are set at 500, or a medium level of control. Tasks that have lower priority are delayed or split before those that have higher priority.

The Resource Leveling Dialog Box

You will find all of the leveling controls in the **Level** group on the **Resource** tab of the ribbon. You can control how Project levels resources by setting the options in the **Resource Leveling** dialog box.

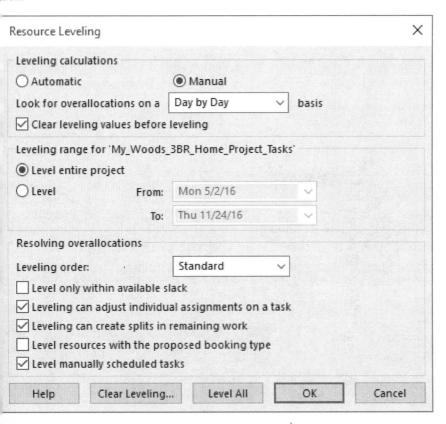

Figure 4-13: The Resource Leveling dialog box gives you control over Project's automatic leveling features.

The following table describes the features of the **Resource Leveling** dialog box.

Button	Function
Level Selection	This button is only active when you select two or more tasks. When you select this button, the selected tasks will be leveled according to the settings in the **Leveling Options** dialog box.
Level Resource	When you select this button, the selected resource will be leveled according to the settings in the **Leveling Options** dialog box.

Button	Function
Level All	When you select this button, all over-allocated resources will be leveled according to the settings in the **Leveling Options** dialog box.
Leveling Options	When you select this button, the **Leveling Options** dialog box will open. There are many options from which you can choose: • You can change **Leveling calculations** from **Manual** to **Automatic** and vice versa. • You can change the time units used to identify over-allocations. The default is **Day by Day,** but you can select **Minute by Minute, Hour by Hour, Week by Week,** or **Month by Month.** • You can choose whether to clear old leveling values before new ones are applied. • You can choose whether to level for the entire duration of the project or only for a specific period of time. • You can choose which rules are followed when resolving over-allocations. After you change the desired options, remember to select **OK.**
Clear Leveling	When you select this button, any leveling you previously applied to the project will be undone. If you select two or more tasks before selecting this button, only the leveling for those tasks will be undone.
Next Overallocation	When you select this button, Microsoft Project Professional 2016 finds the next over-allocated resource.

The Leveling Gantt Chart

When you use Project's automatic leveling feature, many changes may be made to the project plan. It is useful to review these changes using the *Leveling Gantt Chart.* The **Leveling Gantt Chart** is a special view which compares the before and after leveling project plans. Each task will appear with two different colored bars, one for the position before leveling and one for after. You can also review the delay caused by leveling by examining the **Leveling Delay** column. If you are not satisfied with the changes made by automatic leveling, you can undo them and make adjustments in the **Resource Leveling** dialog box to try again, or you can identify which tasks may need manual adjustments.

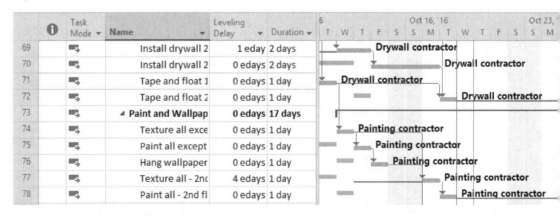

Figure 4-14: Review the changes made by automatic leveling in the Leveling Gantt Chart.

 Access the Checklist tile on your CHOICE Course screen for reference information and job aids on How to Resolve Resource Conflicts.

ACTIVITY 4-5
Resolving Resource Conflicts

Data File

C:\91062Data\Managing Project Plan Resources\Woods_3BR_Home_Project_Level.mpp

Before You Begin

Microsoft Project 2016 is open.

Scenario

You have assigned resources to your tasks. Now you need to make sure that your resources are not overallocated so that they have the time to get the work done. You use various methods to resolve any conflicts.

---

1. Open the **Woods_3BR_Home_Project_Level.mpp** project plan file.

   a) Select **File→Open**.
   b) In the **Open** backstage, select **Browse**.
   c) In the **Open** dialog box, navigate to the **C:\91062Data\Managing Project Plan Resources** folder containing your class files.
   d) Select **Woods_3BR_Home_Project_Level.mpp** and select **Open**.

2. Manually resolve conflicts with **Team Planner** view.

   a) Select **Resource→Team Planner** to open **Team Planner** view.
   b) In the **Resource Name** column, locate the **Inspector** resource.
   c) Scroll to the right in the schedule pane to **Tue Oct 25** and locate the overallocated tasks (you may need to zoom in):

   - Conduct rough-in plumbing inspection
   - Conduct rough-in electrical inspection

   d) Drag the **Conduct rough-in electrical inspection** task to the right in the schedule and drop it in the column for **Wed Oct 26**.

3. Manually resolve conflicts with **Task Inspector.**

    a) In the **View Bar,** select **Gantt Chart.**

    b) In the **Task Entry** table, locate the **42 - Install 1st floor sheathing** task.

    c) In the **Indicators** column, right-click the overallocation (burning man) icon, and then select **Fix in Task Inspector.**

    d) In the **Task Inspector** pane, note the reason for the overallocation: **Resources overallocated due to work on other tasks: Framing contractor.**

    e) Select **Reschedule Task.**

    f) Close **Task Inspector.**

4. Resolve conflicts using **Level Resource.**

    a) On the ribbon, select **Resource→Leveling Options.**

    b) In the **Resource Leveling** dialog box, check the **Level only within available slack** check box. Ensure that the other options are set as follows:

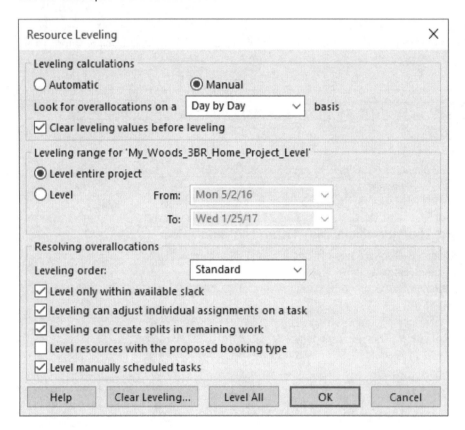

    c) Select **OK.**

    d) In the **Task Entry** table, select **6 - Place Containers.**

    e) Select **Resource→Level Resource.**

    f) In the **Level Resources** dialog box, in the **Selected Resources** list, select **Gary Clark** and verify that **Container** is not selected.

    g) Select **Level Now.**

    h) In the **Microsoft Project** dialog box, review the message about Gary Clark. Select **Skip.** Repeat until the dialog box closes.

    i) On the ribbon, select **Resource→Leveling Options.**

j) In the **Resource Leveling** dialog box, uncheck the **Level only within available slack** check box. Ensure that the other options are set as follows:

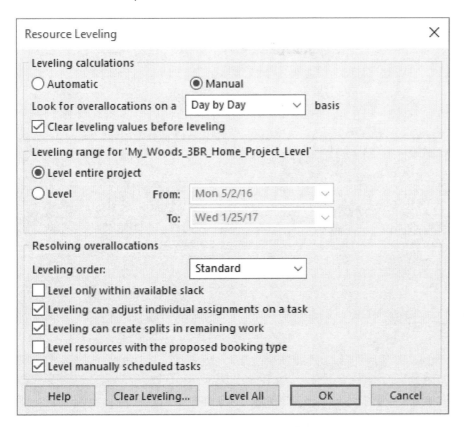

k) Select **OK**.
l) In the **Task Entry** table, select **6 - Place Containers**.
m) Select **Resource→Level Resource**.
n) In the **Level Resources** dialog box, in the **Selected Resources** list, select **Gary Clark** and verify that **Container** is not selected.
o) Select **Level Now**.
p) Verify the changes in the Gantt chart.

5. Resolve remaining conflicts using **Level All**.

a) Select **Level All**.
b) Select the **View** tab.
c) In the **Task Views** grouping, select **Other Views**, and then select **More Views**.
d) In the **More Views** dialog box, select **Leveling Gantt**, and then select **Apply**.
e) Review the changes to the task schedules by examining the values in the **Leveling Delay** column and the Gantt chart.

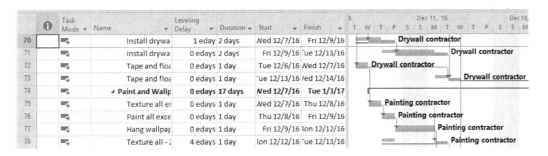

6. Save your changes to **My_Woods_3BR_Home_Project_Level.mpp** and then close the file.

   a) Select **File→Save**.
   b) Select **File→Close**.

Summary

In this lesson, you managed project resources in a number of ways using the **Resources Information** dialog box. You also leveled over-allocated resources in your project.

Which features of the Resource Information dialog box are you most likely to use during your next project?

Which leveling methods will you use during your next project, and why?

Note: Check your CHOICE Course screen for opportunities to interact with your classmates, peers, and the larger CHOICE online community about the topics covered in this course or other topics you are interested in. From the Course screen you can also access available resources for a more continuous learning experience.

5 | Finalizing a Project Plan

Lesson Time: 1 hour

Lesson Introduction

You have created a project plan by creating a work breakdown structure and adding the resources needed to complete the project. Now that you have a plan, you need to review it to see if it meets your needs. Often, a first attempt at the project plan stretches beyond a key deadline or has areas that can be optimized to decrease work and cost. Finally, you will need to prepare for executing the project and share your final plan with stakeholders and team members.

Lesson Objectives

In this lesson, you will finalize a project plan. You will:

- Optimize the project plan using the critical path.

- Set the project baseline and describe how the baseline fields are used.

- Share the project plan with team members and stakeholders.

TOPIC A

Optimize a Project Plan

Every task is important, but those tasks that directly determine the total duration of the project are especially critical. In this topic, we will discuss how to identify those tasks and then modify them to optimize the overall project plan..

The Critical Path

The *critical path* is the longest path of linked tasks in a project, calculated by summing the durations of the individual tasks in the path, that determines the duration of the project. The critical tasks drive the end date of the project.

In other words, the project duration cannot be shorter than the total duration of the tasks in the critical path. Generally, a project has a single critical path, but may have more than one.

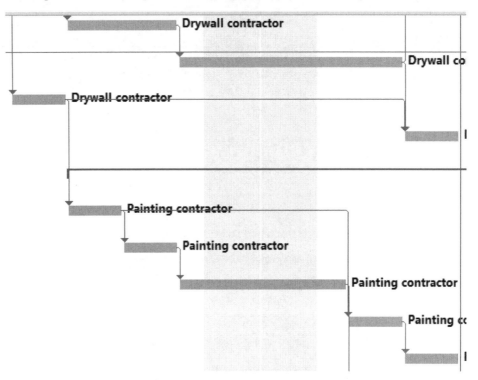

Figure 5-1: The critical path defines the overall project duration.

Project 2016 automatically calculates the critical path for you. In both the **Gantt Chart** and **Network Diagram** views, tasks on the critical path are depicted in red.

Figure 5-2: The critical path displays in red in a network diagram.

Note: If the critical path is not showing up in red in your version of Project 2016, you probably need to change a setting. On the ribbon, select the **Format** tab, find the **Bar Styles** command group, and check the **Critical Tasks** check box.

Methods of Optimizing a Project Plan

Once you understand your project's critical path, you can make changes to the tasks and assignments of the path to optimize the overall project plan. For example, if a task is causing the duration to extend beyond a goal end date, you can add resources or modify the dependencies of the task. You may be able to shorten the duration of a task by adding another person to complete the task. Or, you may realize that a task can start sooner than the finish date of its predecessor. If you have resources that are dedicated to your project, you may wish to review their assignments to see if there are times when they are not working on a task and can be assigned to help on a task on the critical path. You may also want to review those resources which are scarce or expensive to optimize their usage. Finally, you may decide to reduce the scope of the project and remove or shorten some tasks as a result.

- Shorten critical path by:
    - Adding resources
    - Refining dependencies
    - Reassigning tasks
    - Removing tasks/reducing scope
- Optimize resource usage by:
    - Balancing work across resources
    - Minimizing expensive resources

Figure 5-3: Review these methods to optimize your project plan.

Note: After you build your plan and Project calculates the schedule and cost for the project, in rare instances you might have more time or an increased budget. You can choose to end the project ahead of schedule or under budget. Or, with stakeholder approval, you can increase the scope and add quality to the project deliverables.

Effort-Driven Tasks

In an *effort-driven* task, the work required to complete the task is constant even if the number of resources is changed. For example, packing boxes is a task that could be shortened by adding additional resources, but the amount of work (effort) will not change. Not all tasks are effort driven.

For example, when you bake a cake, the amount of time that the cake needs to bake in the oven cannot be changed by adding resources. You can decide for each task whether it should be effort-driven or not.

Duration vs. Work

In project management, duration and work are not the same thing. *Duration* is the number of working time periods (seconds, minutes, hours, days, weeks, months, years) from the beginning of a task until its end. *Work* is the duration of a task multiplied by the level of effort by the resources assigned to the task. For example, if the task "Write grant proposal" has a duration of 5 days, and the resource "Emma" will give 75% of her effort to the task, then the work is 3.75 days.

For tasks that require a fixed amount of work, the duration of the task can be decreased by adding more level of effort by resources. For example, if the task "Debug program" has a duration of 10 days and a single programmer is assigned to the task at a 100% level of effort, then assigning another programmer to the same task at a 100% level of effort should reduce the duration of the task to 5 days.

 Access the Checklist tile on your CHOICE Course screen for reference information and job aids on How to Optimize Duration.

ACTIVITY 5-1
Optimizing a Project Plan

Data File
C:\91062Data\Finalizing a Project Plan\Woods_3BR_Home_Project_Optimize.mpp

Before You Begin
Microsoft Project 2016 is open.

Scenario
You've modified your project plan and resolved the resource conflicts, but now your project finish date is coming in after the end of the year. You need to understand the critical path and make changes so that you can meet your December 31, 2016 deadline. Also, the concrete contractor has agreed to add another resource to double their effort. They still want you to hold off on building the backyard fence so they can get the trucks into the backyard to finish pouring the patio. After seeing how that impacts the plan, you think you can tighten up some of the durations and dependencies. Thankfully, you've been informed that another volunteer will be able to drive the truck so you can relieve Gary Clark if needed. Also, you find out that you don't have to wait on building the fence until the appliances are delivered since that truck is much smaller. You make the necessary adjustments to optimize the plan.

1. Open the **Woods_3BR_Home_Project_Optimize.mpp** project plan file.
   a) Select **File→Open**.
   b) In the **Open** backstage, select **Browse**.
   c) In the **Open** dialog box, navigate to the **C:\91062Data\Finalizing a Project Plan** folder containing your class files.
   d) Select **Woods_3BR_Home_Project_Optimize.mpp** and select **Open**.

2. Display the critical path.
   a) In the **View Bar**, select **Gantt Chart**.
   b) On the ribbon, select the **View** tab.
   c) On the ribbon, in the **Highlight** drop-down list, select **Critical**.
   d) On the ribbon, select **Format**.
   e) In the **Bar Styles** group, check the **Critical Tasks** check box.
   f) Review the highlighted tasks to understand what is driving the end date of the project.

3. Add resources to tasks assigned to the **Concrete contractor** resource.
   a) On the **View Bar**, select **Resource Sheet**.
   b) Locate the **Concrete contractor** resource.
   c) In the row for the **Concrete contractor**, in **Max. Units** column, enter *200%*
   d) In the **View Bar**, select **Gantt Chart**.
   e) Locate and select the following tasks:
      - 23-Form basement
      - 24-Place concrete for foundations & basement
      - 26-Strip basement wall forms
      - 27-Waterproof/ins basement
   f) On the ribbon, select **Resource→Assign Resources**.

g) In the **Assign Resources** dialog box, in the **Concrete contractor** row, in the **Units** column, enter *200%*

h) Repeat steps **e** through **g** for the following tasks:
- 55-Place concrete for basement floor
- 106-Pour concrete driveway and sidewalks

i) In the **Assign Resources** dialog box, select **Close**.

4. Revise the length of a critical task.

a) Double-click the **2- Finalize plans and develop estimate with owner, architect** task.

b) In the **Task Information** dialog box, select the **Advanced** tab.

c) Uncheck **Effort driven**.

d) In the **Duration** field, enter *10 days*

e) Select **OK** to close the **Task Information** dialog box.

5. Reassign tasks.

a) In the **Task Entry** table, select the following tasks:
- 6-Place Containers
- 8-Haul Recycling
- 9-Haul Waste

a) Select **Resource→Assign Resources**.

b) In the **Assign Resources** dialog box, select **Gary Clark**.

c) Select **Replace**.

d) In the **Replace Resource** dialog box, in the **With** table, select **Volunteer 4**.

e) Select **OK** .

f) Select **Close** to close the **Assign Resources** dialog box.

6. Change a dependency to shorten the critical path.

a) Locate the **107-Install Backyard Fence** task.

b) In the row for task **107-Install Backyard Fence**, in the **Predecessors** column, change it to read *106*

7. Save the file as **My_Woods_3BR_Home_Project_Optimize.mpp** and close it.

a) On the ribbon, select **File→Save As**.

b) Select **Browse** and then navigate to **C:\091062Data\Finalizing a Project Plan**.

c) In the **File name** field, enter *My_Woods_3BR_Home_Project_Optimize* and then select **Save**.

d) Select **File→Close**.

TOPIC B

Set a Baseline

When you are moving from project planning to project execution, it's a good idea to set a baseline so that you can measure how well your project is performing. In this topic, you'll discuss baselines and how to set them.

Baselines

A *baseline* is a measurement, calculation, or location used as a basis for comparison. A *project baseline* is an approved plan for a project. Normally the project plan is approved by the *project sponsor* (the person in an organization who authorizes, supports, and approves a project). The baseline is a snapshot of the planned scope, time, and cost of a project. As the project is executed, you can compare actual scope, time, and cost against the baseline to measure how the project is performing. Here are some of the questions that can be answered.

Project Area	Monitoring Questions
Scope	• Are we doing the tasks we planned to do? • Are we doing more or different tasks than anticipated? • Are we doing fewer tasks than anticipated?
Time	• Are we behind schedule? • Are we on schedule? • Are we ahead of schedule?
Cost	• Are we under budget? • Are we on budget? • Are we over budget?

If your project is not performing as expected, you can take corrective action to finish the project according to scope, on time, and within budget. This is the monitoring and controlling function of project management.

The Baseline Table

Project 2016 enables you set up to 11 baselines. The best practice is to use **Baseline** (without a number) for the project plan when it is initially approved, and then to use **Baseline 1–10** when the project sponsor approves later changes to the project plan. For example, if the project sponsor approves the addition of several new project tasks a month into project execution, you should capture the change by setting Baseline 1. The *Baseline table* displays the values for the five most commonly used default **Baseline** fields.

In Project, a baseline is a group of nearly 20 primary reference points (in five categories: start dates, finish dates, durations, work, and cost estimates) that you can set to record the original project plan when that plan is completed and refined. As the project progresses, you can set additional baselines (to a total of 11 for each project) to help measure changes in the plan. For example, if your project has several phases, you can save a separate baseline at the end of each phase, to compare planned values against actual data.

	Task Name	Baseline Dur.	Baseline Start	Baseline Finish	Baseline Work	Baseline Cost
0	◢ **Woods Family 3BR Home**	**166.5 days**	**Mon 5/2/16**	**Wed 12/28/16**	**2,107.2 hrs**	**$183,680.00**
1	◢ General Condition	45 days	Mon 5/2/16	Tue 7/5/16	507.2 hrs	$183,280.00
2	Finalize plans a	10 days	Mon 5/2/16	Fri 5/13/16	99.2 hrs	$0.00
3	Sign contract an	1 day	Mon 5/16/16	Mon 5/16/16	32 hrs	$0.00
4	◢ Clear Old Home	24 days	Wed 6/1/16	Tue 7/5/16	376 hrs	$3,280.00
5	Demolition o	10 days	Wed 6/1/16	Tue 6/14/16	80 hrs	$0.00
6	Place Contair	1 day	Wed 6/1/16	Wed 6/1/16	24 hrs	$40.00
7	Sort Debris	5 days	Thu 6/9/16	Wed 6/15/16	240 hrs	$200.00
8	Haul Recyclin	1 day	Tue 7/5/16	Tue 7/5/16	16 hrs	$20.00
9	Haul Waste	1 day	Thu 6/16/16	Thu 6/16/16	16 hrs	$3,020.00

Figure 5-4: You can view the current Baseline values in the Baseline table.

Because the baseline provides the reference points against which you compare actual project progress, the baseline should include your best estimates for task duration, start and finish dates, costs, and other project variables that you want to monitor. The baseline may also represent a contractual obligation for the project. Baseline information that consistently differs from current data may indicate that your original plan is no longer accurate, possibly because the scope needs review or because the nature of the project has changed. If project stakeholders agree that the difference warrants it, you can modify or rework the baseline at any time during the project. You may find that setting multiple baselines is especially useful for long projects or for projects in which the baseline is rendered irrelevant by significant changes to scheduled tasks or costs.

The Set Baseline Dialog Box

You can easily set a project baseline by selecting the **Project** tab on the ribbon, finding the **Schedule** command group, selecting the **Set Baseline** button, and selecting the **Set Baseline** option.

Selecting this option will display the **Set Baseline** dialog box.

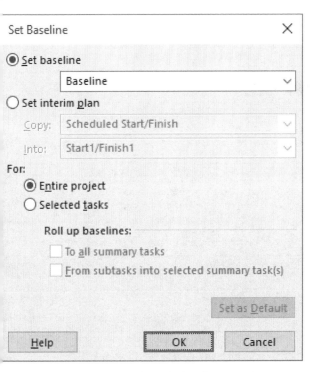

 Note: As a project manager, you should have a clearly defined process for evaluating and approving changes to the project baseline. The positive and negative effects of potential changes to project scope, time, or cost must be carefully considered before implementing them.

 Access the Checklist tile on your CHOICE Course screen for reference information and job aids on How to Set a Baseline.

ACTIVITY 5-2
Setting a Baseline

Data File

C:\91062Data\Finalizing a Project Plan\Woods_3BR_Home_Project_Finalize.mpp

Before You Begin

Microsoft Project 2016 is open.

Scenario

Now that you have optimized your project plan and you have a plan that completes before the end-of-year deadline, it's time to save the baseline so that you can compare progress against the plan as you execute the project. You create a new baseline.

1. Open the **Woods_3BR_Home_Project_Finalize.mpp** project plan file.
   a) Select **File→Open**.
   b) In the **Open** backstage, select **Browse**.
   c) In the **Open** dialog box, navigate to the **C:\91062Data\Finalizing a Project Plan** folder containing your class files.
   d) Select **Woods_3BR_Home_Project_Finalize.mpp** and select **Open**.

2. Display the **Baseline** table.
   a) Right-click the **Select Table** button (the empty area in the top left of the **Task Entry** table.)

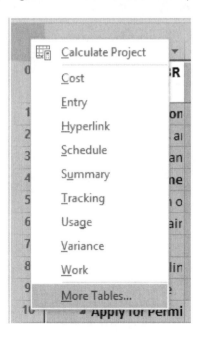

   b) Select **More Tables**.
   c) In the **More Tables** dialog box, select **Baseline** and then select **Apply**.
   d) Verify that the **Baseline** table appears.

e) Verify the empty values in the **Baseline** fields.

Task Name	Baseline Dur.	Baseline Start	Baseline Finish	Baseline Work	Baseline Cost
0 ▲ **Woods Family 3BR Home**	**0 days**	**NA**	**NA**	**0 hrs**	**$0.00**
1 ◢ **General Condition**	**0 days**	**NA**	**NA**	**0 hrs**	**$0.00**
2 Finalize plans ai	0 days	NA	NA	0 hrs	$0.00
3 Sign contract an	0 days	NA	NA	0 hrs	$0.00
4 ◢ **Clear Old Home**	**0 days**	**NA**	**NA**	**0 hrs**	**$0.00**
5 Demolition o	0 days	NA	NA	0 hrs	$0.00
6 Place Contair	0 days	NA	NA	0 hrs	$0.00

3. Set a baseline for the current plan.

a) On the **Project** ribbon, select **Set Baseline**, and then select **Set Baseline** from the menu.
b) In the **Set Baseline** dialog box, verify that **Set Baseline** is selected and **Entire Project** is selected.
c) Select **OK**.
d) Verify the values in the **Baseline** table.

Task Name	Baseline Dur.	Baseline Start	Baseline Finish	Baseline Work	Baseline Cost
0 ◢ **Woods Family 3BR Home**	**165 days**	**Mon 5/2/16**	**Tue 12/27/16**	**2,107.2 hrs**	**$183,680.00**
Project Budget		*NA*	*NA*		
1 ◢ **General Conditions**	**45 days**	**Mon 5/2/16**	**Tue 7/5/16**	**507.2 hrs**	**$183,280.00**
Construction Fixed		*Mon 5/2/16*	*Tue 7/5/16*		*$180,000.00*
2 ◢ Finalize plans and d	10 days	Mon 5/2/16	Fri 5/13/16	99.2 hrs	$0.00
General contrac		*Mon 5/2/16*	*Fri 5/13/16*	*40 hrs*	*$0.00*
Architect		*Mon 5/2/16*	*Fri 5/13/16*	*40 hrs*	*$0.00*
Owner		*Mon 5/2/16*	*Fri 5/13/16*	*9.6 hrs*	*$0.00*
Mortgage lende		*Mon 5/2/16*	*Fri 5/13/16*	*9.6 hrs*	*$0.00*
3 ◢ Sign contract and nc	1 day	Mon 5/16/16	Mon 5/16/16	32 hrs	$0.00
General contrac		*Mon 5/16/16*	*Mon 5/16/16*	*8 hrs*	*$0.00*
Architect		*Mon 5/16/16*	*Mon 5/16/16*	*8 hrs*	*$0.00*
Owner		*Mon 5/16/16*	*Mon 5/16/16*	*8 hrs*	*$0.00*
Mortgage lende		*Mon 5/16/16*	*Mon 5/16/16*	*8 hrs*	*$0.00*
4 ◢ **Clear Old Home**	**24 days**	**Wed 6/1/16**	**Tue 7/5/16**	**376 hrs**	**$3,280.00**
5 ◢ Demolition of Ol	10 days	Wed 6/1/16	Tue 6/14/16	80 hrs	$0.00
Site excavatic		*Wed 6/1/16*	*Tue 6/14/16*	*80 hrs*	*$0.00*
6 ◢ Place Containers	1 day	Wed 6/1/16	Wed 6/1/16	24 hrs	$40.00
Volunteer 4		*Wed 6/1/16*	*Wed 6/1/16*	*8 hrs*	*$0.00*
Container		*Wed 6/1/16*	*Wed 6/1/16*	*16 hrs*	*$40.00*
7 ◢ Sort Debris	5 days	Thu 6/9/16	Wed 6/15/16	240 hrs	$200.00
Volunteer 1		*Thu 6/9/16*	*Wed 6/15/16*	*40 hrs*	*$0.00*
Volunteer 2		*Thu 6/9/16*	*Wed 6/15/16*	*40 hrs*	*$0.00*

4. Save the file as **My_Woods_3BR_Home_Project_Finalize.mpp** and close it.

a) On the ribbon, select **File→Save As**.
b) Select **Browse** and then navigate to **C:\091062Data\Finalizing a Project Plan**.
c) In the **File name** field, enter *My_Woods_3BR_Home_Project_Finalize* and then select **Save**.
d) Select **File→Close**.

TOPIC C

Share a Project Plan

Once you draft a project plan, you will need to deliver it to your project stakeholders for review and to your project sponsor for approval. In this topic, you will use several methods for delivering project plans.

Printed Project Plans

You can print any view on the **View** bar. The **Gantt Chart** view is the one most often shared in paper format, but you may find it useful to print other project views—especially the **Calendar** and **Network Diagram** views.

Before you print a view, you may want to change the amount of detail that will be displayed. You can do this by:

- Hiding subtasks
- Hiding columns
- Resizing the panes of a view
- Changing the zoom level

 Note: Remember that you can select **View→Entire Project** to see the entire time scale in a view.

Once the view is adjusted to your desired detail amount and zoom level, you can start printing by selecting the **File** tab on the ribbon and then selecting the **Print** tab on the **Backstage.** The first thing you will probably notice on the **Print** screen is the large **Print Preview** area in the right pane, which shows you exactly how the printed page will look. In the bottom-right corner of the **Print Preview** pane you will find several controls for navigating and zooming the preview.

Print

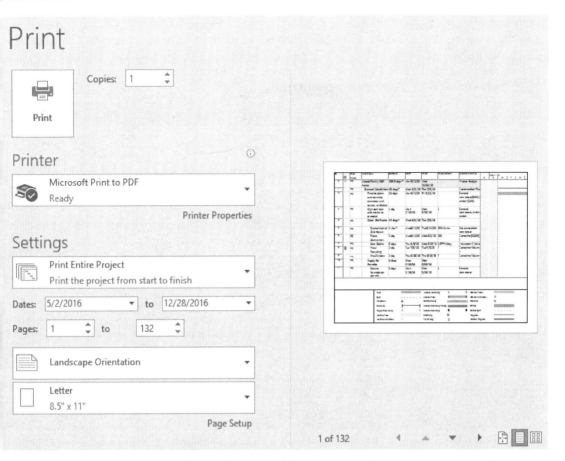

Figure 5-6: The Print screen on the Backstage enables you to preview your current settings before you print.

If you are not satisfied with the preview, you can change the **Settings** options in the left pane of the **Print** tab. You can choose to print:

- The entire project.
- Specific dates.
- Specific pages.
- In landscape or portrait page orientation.
- A variety of page sizes.

If you select the **Page Setup** link, a **Page Setup** dialog box will open that gives you many more options grouped into six tabs. These include the margins, header, footer, and legend.

When the **Print Preview** looks like you want, you can select a printer and select the **Print** button.

 Access the Checklist tile on your CHOICE Course screen for reference information and job aids on How to Print a Project View.

Syncing Project Plans with SharePoint

If your organization uses Microsoft SharePoint, you can synchronize your Microsoft Project Professional task list with a SharePoint task list. Project team members can view the schedule on SharePoint. When they update their work progress on SharePoint, you will see their changes in Project. Conversely, any changes you make in Project will be updated on SharePoint so that team members can see them.

When you select the **Sync with SharePoint** button on the **Share** screen, you will be prompted to go to the **Save As** screen. When you select the **Sync with SharePoint** button on the **Save As** screen, you will have the option of syncing with a new SharePoint site or an existing one. In ether case you will need a valid SharePoint **Site address, User Name,** and **Password.**

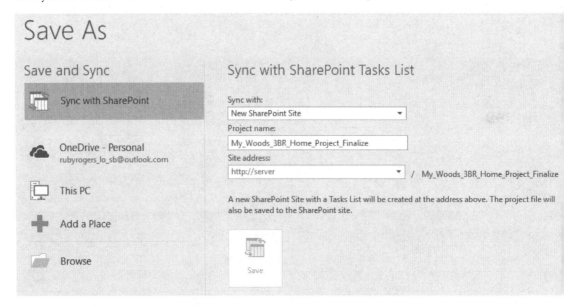

Figure 5–7: Syncing with SharePoint is integrated into the Save As screen.

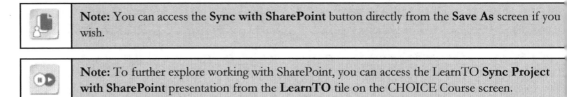

Note: You can access the **Sync with SharePoint** button directly from the **Save As** screen if you wish.

Note: To further explore working with SharePoint, you can access the LearnTO **Sync Project with SharePoint** presentation from the **LearnTO** tile on the CHOICE Course screen.

Emailing Project Plans

From the **Share** screen you can also email the Project file to one or more people. When you select the **Email** button and then the **Send as Attachment** button, a new Microsoft Outlook email message will be generated with a copy of the Project file as an attachment. However, be aware that recipients must have a version of Microsoft Project or a third-party Microsoft Project viewer installed on their computers to view the attachment.

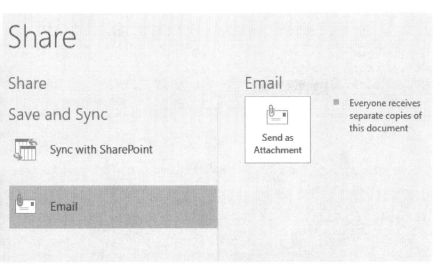

Figure 5-8: You can email a project from the Share screen.

 Note: To further explore sharing Project 2016 files by email, you can access the LearnTO **Share Project 2016 Files by Email** presentation from the **LearnTO** tile on the CHOICE Course screen.

File Formats

The standard file format for a project plan is the .mpp file, which stands for Microsoft Project Plan. While Project 2016 can open .mpp files from all previous versions of Microsoft Project, people using earlier versions of Project will not be able to open Project 2016 .mpp files. You can save your project plan in earlier file formats (also referred to as legacy formats). You can choose from the available file formats in the **Save As** dialog box.

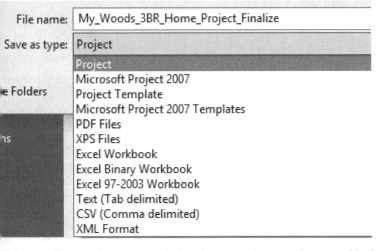

Figure 5-9: Use the Save As dialog box to select an alternate file format.

 Access the Checklist tile on your CHOICE Course screen for reference information and job aids on How to Share a Project Plan.

ACTIVITY 5–3
Sharing a Project Plan

Data File

C:\91062Data\Finalizing a Project Plan\Home_move_plan_handout.mpp

Before You Begin

Microsoft Project 2016 is open.

Scenario

You have a project plan file for a home move. You want to share it as a handout with the Woods family and other families to use as a guideline for preparing to move into their new home. You will prepare the file for printing by scheduling the project from the end date to correspond with the targeted move-in date, prepare the view of the plan, and print it.

1. Open the **Home_move_plan_handout.mpp** project plan file.

   a) Select **File→Open**.

   b) In the **Open** backstage, select **Browse**.

   c) In the **Open** dialog box, navigate to the **C:\91062Data\Finalizing a Project Plan** folder containing your class files.

   d) Select **Home_move_plan_handout.mpp** and select **Open**.

2. Customize the project plan for printing.

   a) On the ribbon, select **Project→Project Information**.

   b) In the **Project Information** dialog box, in the **Schedule from** drop-down list, select **Project Finish Date**.

   c) In the **Finish date** date field, select or enter *1/2/2017*.

   d) Select **OK**.

   e) Select **View→Zoom→Entire Project** to fit the entire Gantt chart in the view.

   f) Resize the **Task Entry** table so that the columns appear as below.

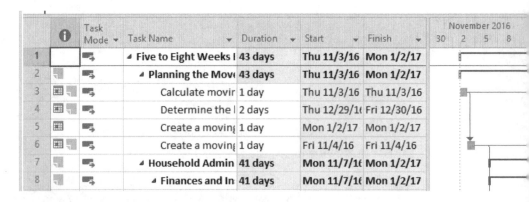

3. Print the project plan.

   a) On the **Quick Access Toolbar**, select **Print Preview**.

   b) On the **Print** screen, in the **Printer** drop-down list, select **Microsoft XPS Document Writer**.

    c) Select **Print**.

    d) In the **Save Print Output As** dialog box, in the **File Name** field, enter *my_printout* and select **Save**.

    e) Monitor the progress in the **Printing** dialog box.

4. Close the **Home_move_plan_handout.mpp** file without saving the changes.

    a) Select **File→Close**.

    b) In the **Microsoft Project** dialog box, select **No** to discard the changes.

Summary

In this lesson, you optimized and delivered a Microsoft Project Professional 2016 plan on paper and in several electronic formats.

Which view(s) of your next project plan are you most likely to print, and why?

Why should you optimize the project plan?

 Note: Check your CHOICE Course screen for opportunities to interact with your classmates, peers, and the larger CHOICE online community about the topics covered in this course or other topics you are interested in. From the Course screen you can also access available resources for a more continuous learning experience.

Course Follow-Up

Congratulations! You have completed the *Microsoft® Project 2016: Part 1* course. You successfully drafted and shared a project plan.

Businesses, academic institutions, and other organizations conduct various projects to develop products, improve processes, and meet organizational goals. There is a growing demand for professionals like you to manage these project successfully. The ability to complete projects on time, within budget, and according to specifications is crucial for all professionals—regardless of whether project management is an official part of your duties. Creating and sharing well-developed project plans will help you meet these goals while keeping your project running smoothly. Microsoft Project Professional 2016 is a powerful tool that can enable you to plan projects effectively and efficiently.

What's Next?

Microsoft® Project 2016: Part 2 is the next course in this series. In that course, you will learn the advanced features of Microsoft Project Professional 2016—such as capturing progress of executing projects, customizing Project using templates and views, and creating reports. You will also perform higher-level analysis of a project's progress and apply strategies to keep the project on track.

You are encouraged to explore Project further by actively participating in any of the social media forums set up by your instructor or training administrator through the **Social Media** tile on the CHOICE Course screen.

Solutions

ACTIVITY 1–1: Identifying Project Management Concepts

1. True or False? A project is a series of steps performed to reach a specific goal.
   - ☑ True
   - ☐ False

2. The scope, the tasks involved, and the resources required for a project are all defined during which process group?
   - ○ Executing
   - ○ Monitoring and Controlling
   - ○ Closing
   - ◉ Planning

3. What is the importance of monitoring a project?

   A: The importance of monitoring a project is to track the project's progress against the original plan so that you can take corrective actions to keep the project on track.

4. True or False? Project management is the application of knowledge, skills, tools, and techniques to accomplish activities or tasks to meet the objectives set for a project.
   - ☑ True
   - ☐ False

5. Which project management process group involves the completion of tasks and the coordination of people and other resources to carry out the plan?
   - ○ Initiating
   - ◉ Executing
   - ○ Planning
   - ○ Closing

6. **Who is the project sponsor?**

   A: The project sponsor is the person who has the authority to approve or terminate the project.

7. **Which of the following are considered the classic triple constraints?**

   - ☑ Scope
   - ☑ Cost
   - ☐ Earned Value
   - ☑ Time
   - ☐ Space

8. **What is scope creep?**

   A: Scope creep is the gradual addition of work which eventually makes the original cost and schedule estimates unachievable.

Glossary

allocation
The scheduling of tasks and resources, taking into account both resource availability and project duration.

Assignment Information dialog box
The dialog box containing all the information about an assignment between a task and a resource grouped into tabs.

auto scheduled
A mode of task scheduling in which Project controls the task's start date, end date, and duration.

Backstage
The central location used for controlling the overall Project program accessed via the File tab.

base calendar
A calendar which can be assigned to a project and on which a resource or task calendar may be based and further refined.

baseline
A measurement, calculation, or other data point used as a basis for comparison.

Baseline table
The table view that displays the information stored in the Baseline fields in a project plan.

budget resource
A special type of cost resource used to track a budget at the project level.

Change Working Time dialog box
The dialog box which enables you to modify the working time for a base calendar.

constraint
A limitation that affects when a task can be scheduled.

contextual tab
The last tab on the ribbon which adapts to what is selected in the view area.

cost resource
A resource used to capture expenses or track a budget.

Create New Base Calendar dialog box
The dialog box which enables you to copy an existing base calendar or create a new one from scratch.

critical path
The longest path of linked tasks in a project that determines the duration and finish date of the project.

deadline
A setting which enables you to track how close a task finish date is to a deadline date.

dependency
A logical relationship between two tasks in which the start or finish of one task affects the start or finish of the other.

duration
The number of working time periods (seconds, minutes, hours, days, weeks, months, years) from the beginning of a task until its end.

effort-driven
When a task is effort driven, Project keeps the total task work at its current value, regardless of how many resources are assigned to the task. When new resources are assigned, remaining work is distributed to them..

exception
In Project 2016, a day or week when working time is different than what is normal for the base calendar.

FF
(Finish-to-Finish) A dependency between two tasks in which the first task must be completed before the second task can be completed.

FS
(Finish-to-Start) A dependency between two tasks in which the first task must be completed before the second task can begin.

Gantt chart
A method for displaying project tasks over time. Named after Henry Gantt, who designed the tool between 1910 and 1915.

import map
The map which defines how data from a source file corresponds to the columns in a Project plan.

Import Wizard
The wizard which walks you through importing data from another program into Project 2016.

lag
A delay between two tasks that are linked together.

lead
An overlap in time between two tasks that are linked together.

leveling
The rescheduling and reassignment of tasks to resolve resource over-allocations.

Leveling Gantt chart
A special Gantt chart view comparing the project plan before and after leveling.

link
In Project 2016, the act or result of joining two tasks together to create a dependency.

manually scheduled
A mode of task scheduling in which you manually control the task's start date, end date, and duration.

material resource
A resource tracked by the amount of units consumed.

milestone
An important point in a project.

over-allocated
When a resource is assigned to do more work on a project than it can do within its normal working capacity.

predecessor
A task that must be started or finished before another task can be performed.

project
A temporary initiative to create a unique result.

project baseline
The collection of baseline measurements that constitute the approved plan for the project.

project calendar
The calendar that determines the overall schedule of a project.

project constraint
Anything that constrains or dictates the actions of the project team.

Project Information dialog box
The dialog box which displays information about the project as a whole such as the start date, calendar, and scheduling mode.

project management
The administration and supervision of projects using a well-defined set of knowledge, skills, tools, and techniques.

project manager
The primary person directing the project's flow and the communication between project participants.

Project Properties dialog box
The dialog box which allows you to enter information to help search and organize your project files such as your name, your manager's name, and keywords about the project.

project sponsor
The person in an organization who authorizes, supports, and approves a project.

project stakeholder
Anyone who is actively involved in a project or has an interest in its outcome.

project template
A special type of project file which contains details for a sample project that you can use as a starting point for a new project.

Quick Access Toolbar
The toolbar in the top left of the Project window which enables access to frequently used commands.

resource
A person, piece of equipment, consumable material, or other cost that is used to accomplish a project task.

resource availability
The availability of the resource specified by start and end dates in the Resource Information dialog box.

resource calendar
A calendar for a particular resource containing exceptions or working time specific to that resource.

Resource Information dialog box
The dialog box which contains all of the information about a resource grouped into tabs.

Resource Sheet
A table view where resources can be viewed, added, and modified.

ribbon
The tabbed area along the top of the Project window containing most of the commands arranged by group.

scope creep
An increase in the project's scope after the plan is set.

SF
(Start-to-Finish) A dependency between two tasks in which the first task must begin before the second task can be completed.

SS
(Start-to-Start) A dependency between two tasks in which the first task must begin before the second task can begin.

status bar
The area at the bottom of the Project window which displays current program settings, shortcuts, and the Zoom control.

subtask
A task that is grouped under a larger summary task.

successor
A task that is logically linked to one or more predecessor tasks.

summary task
A task that has related subtasks grouped below it.

task
A specific chunk of project work.

task constraint
A date-based limitation imposed on a task which constrains the start or finish date.

Task Entry table

The main area in Project from which you view, enter, and modify tasks.

Task Information dialog box

The dialog box containing all the information about a task grouped into tabs.

Task Inspector

A special pane to the left of the view area which provides information about a task's scheduling and offers resolutions to conflicts.

Task Usage table

A table view displaying the task list with assigned resources and planned work under each task.

team member

A person who is responsible for performing or approving the work to complete the project.

Team Planner view

A view of resources and tasks arranged in a schedule grid that can be easily modified using a mouse or touchscreen.

Tell Me bar

The area above the ribbon where you can search for commands and help content.

triple constraint

The three most important factors in a project —scope, time, and cost—which are dynamically linked so that any change in one will impact the others.

Trust Center

The area in the Project settings which controls security and privacy settings such as enabling legacy file formats.

view

A combination of specific tables and/or charts in the main window used by Project to display information relevant to the task at hand.

WBS

(Work Breakdown Structure) The hierarchical arrangement of a task list.

work

The duration of a task multiplied by the level of effort by the resources assigned to the task.

work breakdown structure

A deliverable-oriented outline of a project's work.

work resource

A resource tracked and employed on a time basis.

working time

Whenever labor is being performed on a project, on a task, or by a resource.

Index